MW01057926

# SPORTSMAN'S
# BEST

BOOK & DVD SERIES

FS Books:
**Sport Fish of Florida**
**Sport Fish of the Gulf of Mexico**
**Sport Fish of the Atlantic**
**Sport Fish of Fresh Water**
**Sport Fish of the Pacific**

**Baits, Rigs & Tackle**
**Sportsman's Best: Sailfish**
**Sportsman's Best: Inshore Fishing**
**Sportsman's Best: Snapper & Grouper**
**Annual Fishing Planner**
**The Angler's Cookbook**

**Florida Sportsman Magazine**
**Shallow Water Angler Magazine**
**Florida Sportsman Fishing Charts**
**Lawsticks**
**Law Boatstickers**

Author, George LaBonte
Edited by Joe Richard and Florida Sportsman Staff
Art Director, Drew Wickstrom
Illustrations by Joe Suroviec
Copy Edited by Jerry McBride
Photos by Joe Richard, Bill Combes, William Boyce, Ovi Verona,
    Guy Harvey, Pat Ford, South Fishing, Inc.

www.floridasportsman.com

# SAILFISH

# CONTENTS

**SB**

**SPORTSMAN'S BEST**
**S A I L F I S H**

Ever have one of these guys jump in your face? It's no wonder sailfish have so many die-hard fans.

# Sailfish Put the "S" in Spectacular

If the quality of a sportfish is measured by its performance on the end of the line, no other fish comes close. Sailfish have it all: speed, heart, and an aptitude for aerial stunts that would make a tarpon blush. Ever see a sailfish tail-walk? It's as marvelous a thing as you'll see in nature. That distinctive dorsal fin and powerful, razor-edged tail work magic in, and above, the cobalt currents.

*Istiophorus platypterus* also possesses a mystique that has kept anglers spellbound for many decades. We constantly debate new theories on their migrations, as well as new tackle and strategies for connecting with them.

*Sportsman's Best: Sailfish* is therefore more than just a treatise on angling methods. Written by Capt. George LaBonte of Jupiter, FL, with edit work and photography by Joe Richard, it is aimed at capturing the spirit of a magnificent gamefish. These two fishing authorities, along with Art Director Drew Wickstrom and other editors at Florida Sportsman magazine, have assembled what they believe is the best book on sailfish yet to be published. Hence Sportsman's Best.

In recent decades, anglers have become leaders in conserving sailfish. Threats to the future of the species come in many forms, from high-seas commercial longline fishing to declines in forage due to coastal habitat loss. LaBonte, Richard and all of us at FS believe that informed, inspired fishermen are vital to maintaining populations of the spectacular sailfish.

Be thrilled, be involved.

—Jeff Weakley, Editor, Florida Sportsman

Angler works on a sailfish at boatside, in the propwash.

# You Never Forget Your First Time

They say you never forget your first time. Considering the fact that I had already caught huge bluefin tuna exceeding 1,000 pounds by the time I saw my first sailfish, you might think the event would be anticlimatic. The fact is, I remember every detail: One sunny winter day off South Florida, I was spooling back a Sea Witch and strip bait into a flat calm cobalt ocean. It was the first bait in the water, in fact, and it barely made it beyond the exhaust before a long black snake came up out of nowhere with bad intentions. Since it was my first billfish encounter, I was mesmerized by how wild this fish was as it approached. The fish lit up like a Christmas tree and it was "game on."

So spellbound was I, a seasoned angler, that I scarcely noticed the tugging in my hands. I suddenly remembered what I was actually doing—and that the bait and I were connected. I gained some control of my senses and soon realized that I should be letting go of the line and feeding this offshore warrior.

Too late! That sail was paying closer attention, biting down on the hook and ripping line from the reel, with only my thumb on the spool. The next few seconds were a blur. All I can say is that at some point you have to lock the reel up in gear—but this little detail escaped me at the time. Another key point is that you can't hold a sailfish with only a bare thumb.

The unholy tangle of mono line and the smell of burning skin are still fresh memories. I didn't catch that sailfish, but the fact that a mere 40-pounder could unravel me so completely made a distinct impression which hasn't faded. Many years and countless sailfish later, they still get the adrenaline flowing. Those initial moments of a sailfish bite and jumps just after the hookup create the purest fishing rush you can get, and I highly recommend it. Fair warning, however: it's addictive. I've got the burn scars to prove it.

—George LaBonte

# CHAPTER 1

# Greatest Gamefish

**M**ost people think of sailfishing as a South Florida phenomenon, but these fish are far more widespread than is commonly known. From North Carolina to Texas, these rapier-billed jumpers prowl in depths of 100 feet or more. In the Florida Keys, they'll move in as shallow as 25 feet, easily visible down below, prowling over empty sand bottom.

All Caribbean islands and The Bahamas hold sailfish, along with Central and much of South America. On the Pacific side, much larger sailfish roam from Mexico down to Panama. Often they're so thick, visiting anglers expect to hook 20 or more fish per day. With that many chances, one might as well try the ultimate, hooking big sailfish up to eight feet or bigger with a fly rod.

If you haven't tried catching sailfish, you've clearly been missing out.

Sailfish make other fish look pretty tame. Thanks to a quirk of nature, they're available to small boat crews within a few casts of the beach— whenever wind and local seas cooperate.

# The Working Man's Billfish

**F**ew things compare to the surge of adrenaline we feel at "the moment of truth." That's the moment when all prep work is done, the ocean looks right, baits are perfect. Just when your mind starts to wander, you hear the phrase all anglers love to spit out: "There he is!" A single black shadow pops up behind a flatline, then another on the outrigger bait, another on a teaser, then both teasers! Get another bait in the water—the surface is alive with white water and jumping sailfish, you're covered up and nothing else seems to matter. This scenario plays itself out

**The surface is alive with jumping sailfish. You're covered up and nothing else seems to matter.**

regularly in my backyard and behind my boat, where I spend the majority of my days in search of that next bite. I happen to be fortunate enough to live just minutes away from Florida's famous "Sailfish Alley," where the lure of fast-paced billfish action attracts visitors from around the world every winter.

You might not believe it when you see millions of dollars worth of nautical machinery lining the docks of local marinas, but this is not a sport exclusive to the wealthy.

When sailfish go on a feeding frenzy, all hell can break loose.

Sailfish don't know your net worth and couldn't care less how much your boat costs. Sailfishing is blue-collar billfishing. Luckily for folks who drag their rig down to the

Following a sailfish from a small boat kingfish-style, with the angler staying in the bow area during most of the fight, and the captain driving, when he isn't attending to myriad other duties.

Whoa! Sailfish jumps right at boatside, very close to the boat crew. The guys in small boats catch their share of sailfish on a regular basis, when the weather cooperates.

## Once you launch your first sailfish in the air, you're hooked.

water behind a pickup truck, sailfish prefer to stay reasonably close to the beach, making them very accessible. With a few simple tackle items and a couple of rods, you could probably catch one from a johnboat on the right day. Whether you belong to the johnboat gang, the million-dollar battlewagons, or somewhere in the middle with the center console fast-movers with two or three outboards, it doesn't really matter. Once you launch your first sailfish in the air, you're hooked. If you haven't done it yet, this book will get you there faster. With some easy-to-understand guidelines, you'll be raising those release flags before you know it.

Some anglers set out to catch their first

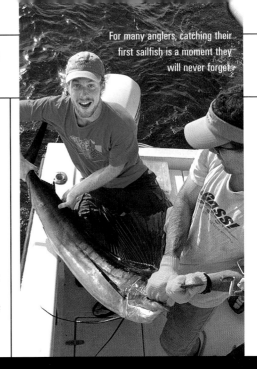

For many anglers, catching their first sailfish is a moment they will never forget.

# Let 'Em Go

The history of fishing for sailfish goes back at least 75 years. Tackle and tactics have changed greatly since then, along with attitudes about the value of sailfish as a renewable resource. If you look at photos

A sailfish battle flag is raised in the harbor, for all to see .

from the past and compare them with today's records, one thing really stands out: Photos of yesteryear include shots of dead sailfish hanging at the dock.

These days, you'll see far more shots of people holding a live fish in the water before the release. This not only makes for a nicer photo (since the fish is more brilliantly colored), but the action of a live shot adds drama to the photo and captures the memory of landing the fish. While it's still legal to kill sailfish for personal consumption, the vast majority of anglers now release all billfish.

A common misconception is that you have to kill a fish for taxidermists to mount them, if you want a trophy for the wall. This is certainly not the case. In fact, marine taxidermists these days seldom use a dead fish for mounting. The modern process involves making a fiberglass mold from a real fish, which can be used many times. They build a perfect replica that can be painted more accurately and will last a lifetime. (We've all seen the old skin mounts in older Florida restaurants, the fish gone

Sailfish have this odd mystique that separates them from all other fish. Anglers can go nuts trying to figure them out.

sailfish and after racking up a few releases, switch to catching tablefare as their new objective. In fact, most folks who live around

dark and peeling, the victim of age and aging oil in the skin). Most taxidermists have a complete assortment of molds to work with, covering all sizes and types of fish, making it a virtual certainty they'll have a mold very close to your fish. Some have up to a hundred sailfish molds alone, that imitate just about anything a sailfish can do.

A dead sailfish brought back to the dock is usually met with off-color comments, dirty looks, even angry frowns. A more proper sign of achievement now are release flags attached to the boat's outrigger lines. A white flag with a sailfish on it flown upside down, or a red triangular pennant symbolizes a released fish. One flag is flown for each fish released, and at the close of the day, your entire crew can enjoy the ritual of filling the 'rigger line with flags, unless they're too tired to bother. (A 20 or 30 sailfish day can cause this phenomenon.)

Billfishing is after all a team effort. On any given day during the winter sailfish run in southeast Florida, you might see strings of red flags lining the riggers at sportfishing docks. Fledgling sailfish anglers may look down the dock with envy at successful crews and work toward their goal of joining the ranks one day. A raised eyebrow or "pretty work" comment from old salts and professional captains on the dock—that's ample reward. SB

sailfish hunting grounds go fishing for the table at some point—but how many of them toss and turn at night, thinking about catching their next snapper? The appeal of sailfish is in simply wanting to look at them. Sailfish have a mystique that can change the tone on a boat unlike other fish. What sets them apart from jacks or sharks? The challenge of tricking sailfish into eating your bait and the thrill of observing the fish's crazy, aerial antics. That's what this is all about. Pound for pound they may not be the toughest fish that swims, but if they lack something in the degree of punishment they dish out, they more than compensate in pure style. With a long, dagger-like bill, and a huge dorsal fin unlike any other in the fish world, they are the embodiment of spectacle. Color changes with mood, from brilliant neon blue to bold silver and black. Sailfish are by far one of our most sought-after gamefish.

Countless bluewater enthusiasts have grown up looking at photos and taxidermy of sailfish caught by their predecessors. Some go back at least to the early days of *Crunch and Des* in the late 1930s, mythical figures who worked out of Miamarina, as related by Miami author Philip Wylie. Many have dreamed when they would get their chance at catching a sailfish. As a younger generation of anglers rise up, the sailfish certainly hasn't lost its appeal. Fortunately, populations of these fish are relatively stable. Their numbers still make it possible to realize a double-digit day, while just offshore. SB

# CHAPTER 2

# The Sailfish

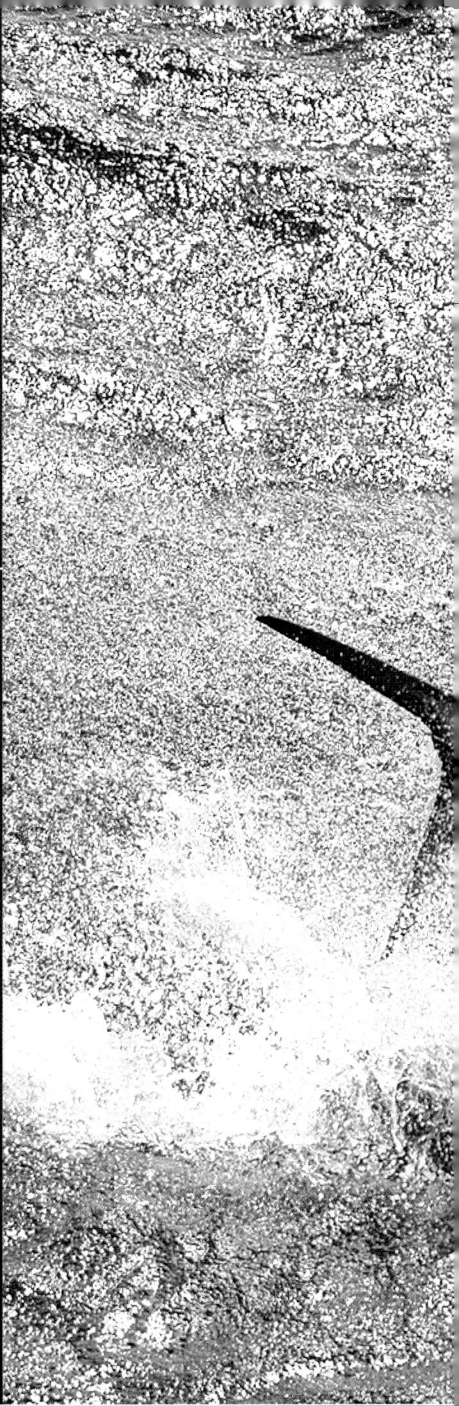

**S**ailfish are a migratory, pelagic billfish ranging throughout the warm waters of the world. Most anglers will quickly agree that these fish are far more graceful and agile than their scientific name of *Istiophorus platypterus*.

Commonly found along near-coastal areas inside of the continental shelf, sailfish live, feed and travel in direct relation to the shape and size of nearby underwater structure. This would also include other factors:

Nearby land masses, the effects of the ocean's tide and current movements, water temperature changes and the abundance of food supply.

**Combine art and science, and you've got a treatise on the amazing sailfish.**

**Joe Richard**

Airborne! In a howling January cold front, this sailfish felt the hook and sprinted for the horizon off Palm Beach. Just one of many fish hooked on a phenomenal day.

# The Amazing Sailfish

S ailfish are perhaps the most widely recognized fish in the non-angling world, as their appearance can't be mistaken for any other fish. Through the popularity of sportfishing for sailfish and the frequent trophy mounts collected by offshore anglers, these are one of the most sought-after of all big game trophies. They decorate walls across the world in homes, marinas, tackle shops and seafood restaurants, and they even provide a novelty prop-like effect in some of the most unlikely settings, such as offices, motels and movie theaters.

The frequent display of these unique fish is what makes sailfish so easily identified by untrained observers. They're highlighted with bright coloring, a spear-like bill and most notably—that exaggerated dorsal fin with the sail-like shape, which earned them their name.

## Sailfish Art

Without question the most popular marine fish painted by artists around the world. Whether chasing ballyhoo on the surface, circling and balling up a school of sardines down deeper, or just jumping in a variety of amazing ways, the sailfish is the king of art. We thought you might enjoy some widely different styles of artistic expression here, while reading about just what it is that really makes the sailfish tick. After all, a better understanding of their life cycle is the key to safe management and conservation.

b.sylvester

Widely available and highly sought-after because of their spectacular aerial performances on light tackle, sailfish are without question the most easily caught member of the billfish clan for bluewater trophy hunters. Certainly the most numerous of all billfish, their schooling behavior on some days makes for multiple encounters—and amazing days. This fact in part accounts for the proliferation of sportfishing boats in any developed area where they're found.

Their popularity as a sport species places a significant and growing importance on their survival as a renewable resource.

Worldwide, however, they are of increasing importance as a commercial food fish and are targeted heavily in waters surrounding less-developed nations. These cash-hungry countries often welcome the small returns they receive, in exchange for allowing other nations with high-tech harvest methods to heavily impact their local fishery. Sailfish are even targeted as a commercial crop in other, more developed areas, often countries that

**Brian Sylvester:**
Moon-lit marauder attacks flying fish, just when they thought they were due for a night's rest.

haven't had the opportunity to utilize or realize this billfish's potential as a sport-oriented, reusable resource.

These facts should be of major concern to billfish anglers in the rest of the world, as little is known about the long-range migrations of sails and other billfish. Though tagging programs have provided us with a glimpse of their possible patterns, it's still hard to predict what effects the exploitation of fish in far-reaching areas of the Caribbean will have on highly valuable stocks off the southeastern United States.

If history repeats itself, as it often does, in a few years we could easily find ourselves wondering what happened to all the sailfish. We may discover that the majority of these

stocks and repair the damage.

The fact there are apparently stable numbers of sailfish around the world should not be mistaken for or used as a license to open up a global market. Sailfish are far too valuable to the economies of a number of countries, to watch them disappear as simple seafood.

## HABITAT

To thrive, sailfish must live within a range of water temperatures that offers comfort and safety. A steady supply of food must also be available. These two factors determine where sailfish will be found along the coast. They're associated with tropical climates and prefer a water temperature range from 72 to 85 degrees. These temperatures can occur as far north as

**Joe Sherk**
Old painting that still hangs over the fireplace at the West Palm Beach Fishing Club. That's the Jupiter Lighthouse in the distance.

fish were harvested, or merely caught and killed unintentionally as bycatch from another fishery. The effects of this over-fishing may not be noticeable to an angling public until the stocks are on the brink of collapse. By then it may be a difficult task to rebuild

southern New Jersey and south all the way to Argentina. Sailfish are found in waters both above and below these latitudes, but temperatures reaching outside of this range are one of the most important factors affecting their movement from one area to another—most

Joe Suroviec
Reaching for the sky on a
perfect day off South Florida.

notably on the lower, or cooler side of their temperature range. Sailfish are simply famous for migrating at the approach of a winter cold front along Florida's Southeast Coast.

The availability of a steady food supply dictates daily movements of sailfish. The near-coastal proliferation of these fish directly revolves around the availability of a ready food

## Sailfish patrol the edges of underwater structures, on the lookout for a quick meal.

supply found over coastal reefs, deep dropoffs and irregular bottom structure. These underwater spots offer shelter and security to the many baitfish comprising a sailfish's daily diet. Different bottom features cause current upwellings and sailfish certainly use these to their advantage. Large quantities of fish, large and small, find these reefs and underwater structures to hide and feed. Sailfish patrol the edges of these bottom structures, on the lookout for a quick meal.

## SAILFISH RESEARCH

In the early 1970s, in response to a growing concern from South Florida anglers, regarding the apparent decline in both number and average size of sailfish landed, the Florida Department of Natural Resources supported research to investigate the status of sailfish stocks off the coast. The research was conducted over a 4-year period by marine biologist John W. Jolley.

Over the course of those four years, Jolley's efforts were mainly focused on the study of age-to-weight and length ratios, and the reproductive processes of sailfish. His research offers sportsmen several useful points to consider, regarding the lifespan of sails as well as their preferred diet. While this book is not a scientific treatise and shouldn't be mistaken for one, some of his research findings can directly benefit sailfish anglers. The following information is provided based largely upon Mr. Jolley's conclusions.

Previous studies conducted on the biology of sailfish indicated they were a fast-growing,

**Russ Smiley**
Sunrise strike to
get your day started.

short-lived fish, with a probable lifespan of about four years. Through modern, more accurate aging techniques and information provided by tag returns of sailfish, it is increasingly apparent that sailfish have a much longer lifespan than previously believed. By analyzing cross sections of dorsal spines taken from sailfish, this research indicates from 149 specimens taken, that ages ranged from one to eight years—with a mean age of approximately four years. Evidence suggests a possible maximum age of up to 12 years. This information dictates a further need to protect the population from over-harvest.

**Kim Rody**
Interpretative
sailfish art.

In the past, it was commonly believed that sailfish of seven feet and weighing 50 pounds were near the end of their life span. It was supposed that killing that fish would not have much of an impact on population stocks. Evidence now suggests a lifespan of twice that length or more, and we realize that a 50-pound fish has several more years to reproduce. Removing too many of them from the overall population (for fish mounts, or as weigh-ins at kill tournaments) would have a potentially far-reaching negative effect on these stocks. This further demonstrates the need for conscious and active protection of the resource for future

generations. It's also a good reason why so few sailfish are brought back to the docks today.

The rapid growth in terms of length previously believed to persist through the short life of the sailfish has in fact been determined to be more prevalent in early stages. It now appears that growth slows progressively with age. As these fish age, they tend to add weight and girth, rather than length. In the first year of life, the sailfish will develop into a fully formed adult fish of five feet or more in length, weighing approximately 15 to 20 pounds. A 4-year-old fish will reach 40 to 50 pounds with a total length of seven feet. This age and size class represents the average catch in the west-

## Growth slows with age. As these fish age, they tend to add weight and girth, rather than length.

ern North Atlantic from the Florida Keys to the Carolinas.

Subsequent years in the life of a sailfish will see a considerable decrease in rate of growth in terms of length, while weight will increase. Consider the difference in length and weight of the seven-foot, 50-pounder compared to a fish of eight and a half feet in length which may weigh as much as 120 pounds. With only a foot and a half increase in length, that fish will gain over 50 pounds of weight.

Sexual maturity is reached in females at about 3 to 4 years of age, at 35 to 45 pounds and at 2 years in males at 15 to 20 pounds.

This estimation is based upon minimum sizes of specimens examined, that contain ripe ovaries and testes. Spawning occurs primarily inshore over shallow sand or rocky bottoms and takes place on the surface, with one or more males accompanying a single female.

Spawning begins as early as April and extends into October, with peak periods of activity during June through August. Jolley's research also suggests that fractional spawning may occur as well.

Based on varying stages of development in ovaries within individual fish examined, he concluded that sailfish may shed three or four

**Guy Harvey**
"Strike Zone" has a number of wide-eyed ballyhoo that suddenly wish they were somewhere else.

batches of eggs over a single spawning season. The conclusion drawn is that sailfish do have a primary spawning season, but due to water temperature and the exact age of the fish, additional spawning may occur whenever conditions are right.

Mature females may carry between 800,000 and 2,000,000 eggs. It would be impossible to speculate how many of that number reach adult size, but certainly, as with most other ocean-dwelling fish that are only one-eighth of an inch in length upon hatching, one would presume that most of these fish succumb to

## At 5 to 10 pounds and just over four feet, they start to appear behind sportfishing boats.

predators shortly after hatching.

At this critical stage in their life it is important for them to eat and stay out of harm's way until they reach a more respectable size. After the first six months, they've passed the most difficult stage of life, and are fully formed sailfish with all of the speed and survival abilities of an adult fish. At 5 to 10 pounds and just over four feet, they start to appear behind the wakes of sportfishing boats, and it is at this stage of their life that fishermen get their first look at them.

As larger, ever-growing adult fish, their need to feed becomes greater all the time. Based on sailfish examined over the four years in Jolley's study, let's look at the stomach contents of these fish and determine the most common food items in a sailfish's diet. Of the 778 fish examined, 530 of them had food items in their stomachs.

Of that number, 71 were found with *Scombridae*, mostly little tunny (bonito in Florida); 63 with *Cephalopoda*, primarily squid; 41 with *Exocoetidae*, or ballyhoo and flying fish; 30 with *Carangidae*, goggle-eyes and blue runners; 25 with *Belonidae*, or needlefish; 25 with *Clupeidae*, or herring (thread herring, sardine and pilchard).

Additionally there was a wide variety of odd marine life including filefish, pipefish, seahorse, dolphin, cutlass fish, butterfish, surgeon-

fish, silverside, anchovies, mojarra, tripletail, snake eel, flounder, grunt, parrotfish, scorpion fish, seabass and sea robin.

That's quite a diversified menu!

This extensive list demonstrates the sailfish

**Jean Eastman**
Pedators compete for ballyhoo.
These dolphin are fairly safe
around sailfish and don't worry
about becoming a meal.

*Jean Eastman*

will feed on an extremely wide variety of species found from the ocean floor to the surface weedlines, and everywhere in between. They do, however, show a distinct preference for the top five on the list. All of the above contents were determined to be food items and not bait used to capture the fish for the study; a good number of the fish examined did in fact have the bait used to catch them still in their stomachs.

**Carey Chen**
Sailfish and tuna working
together, balling up the baitfish.

Sailfish are also known to be primarily daytime feeders, with only occasional nighttime feeding noted around the periods of the full moon.

## DISTRIBUTION

Atlantic sailfish are spread over a wide area, and we have little concrete information on how far-reaching their migration distances may be. It is known, however, that movement tends to be north and south, based on conditions of water temperature, salinity and the availability of food. Looking at a chart of their range, you can see that the movements of fish found in South America's northern extremes are influenced by the South Equatorial Current, which flows north and west to Mexico's Yucatan Peninsula, where it enters the Gulf of Mexico. Sailfish are abundant throughout this range.

On the northeastern side of the Caribbean islands, the North Equatorial Current flows northwest, where it meets the Gulf Stream, which continues north into the Atlantic to the northern extremes of the sailfish's range. In the Eastern Atlantic, off the coast of West Africa, this fish follows the Canary Current north and south, and the North Atlantic Drift as it swings in south over southern Europe.

Because sailfish are found across such a large area, with our knowledge of the movements of the waters they inhabit, we can speculate which fish move where. It is, however, impossible to make an accurate determination without considerably more research.

It's easy to guess that the fish we catch in Mexico go north into the northern Gulf of Mexico, or that the "Sailfish Alley" fish off Southeast Florida go north with the Gulf Stream during summer, or that the Caribbean fish move northwest and southeast, but until we actually know these facts, we must treat the entire population of Atlantic fish as one body, and give them equal protection.

Although it's difficult to enforce conservation rules for such a highly migratory species, it must be done. As has been demonstrated with the western Atlantic bluefin tuna stocks, it makes little sense to manage the fish in one area of its range and rampantly exploit it in another. This practice accomplishes little in the way of keeping fish stocks stable.

Allowing one nation free reign over a commodity while others suffer as stocks are fished down to all-time low levels will hurt us all in the long run.

**Mathew Hardeman**
Pencil drawing., leaping sailfish.

**Pasta Pantaleo**
Sailfish uses its bill to stun flyingfish,
before gulping them down.

# CHAPTER 3

# Sailfish Evolution

**I**f we look back to when the first hook-and-line-caught sailfish was recorded about 100 years ago and compare the past to the present, we see a pattern common to every modern fishery. What started out as a handful of people chasing great numbers of fish has become the opposite: large numbers of anglers chasing what is now only a comparative handful of fish.

Along the way, as the number of fish has diminished, the techniques used to catch these prizes have become, by necessity, more innovative and creative. As a consequence, the fish have become more selective and therefore more difficult to catch. The "highliner" boats (top guns) must always be thinking of new ways to improve their score.

**Sailfish pioneers had time to perfect their sport, but they were breaking new ground.**

The early South Florida sailfish fleet was made up of a motley collection of vessels. The nearest may well have been a harpoon boat from up north. At right is a "blonde bombshell," in the parlance of the 1940s, with a fine pair of Palm Beach sailfish.

# Taking a Trip Back in Time

I often think if I could have one wish, I would love to rig a classic Palm Beach sportfishing boat with state of the art electronics, all the tackle I could fit on board, and with my current knowledge of the sport, be transported back in time to around the 1930s.

Imagine the endless sailfishing possibilities! If I could have a rub on Aladdin's lamp, I'd have my second bait in the water before that lamp hit the ground.

In the early 1900s, fishermen began having regular encounters with sailfish. What began as a nuisance to commercial kingfish trollers soon became a new game to the developing sportfishing crowd in South Florida. The market fishermen of the day had not yet developed any commercial interest in sailfish, so any time spent tangling with them was considered wasted. Tackle was torn up and mackerel were not

Early, innovative anglers figured out how to catch sailfish. Nearby fleet shows that the waters off South Florida could get crowded when the bite was on, even in the 1940s.

being caught. One could argue that time was even wasted on the sailfish. However, the concept of time in 1900 had vastly different meaning from what it does today.

The few sporting boats out there back then had other ideas about sailfish. While trolling for kings, they of course encountered sails. They repeatedly had their baits pulled off the hook or mauled into a useless condition, while rarely hooking the sailfish. What may have begun as a grudge against sailfish by boat crews on these early boats developed into a system to increase hookups.

## The Innovators

Early pioneers of the sport, notably Capts. Charlie Thompson and Bill Hatch, were among the first to notice a peculiar behavioral trait of sailfish. These fish would initially attempt to stun the bait with their bill, and, if allowed some slack line, would soon consume the bait more completely, thereby providing greater chance of a hookup. That's when the dropback was born.

Thompson's early technique was as follows: After setting out the baits, additional line was stripped from the reel, and left on the deck to fall back toward the hook after "yon sail" struck the bait. This was the first dropback technique for catching sailfish with repeatability. Thompson was already on his way to the top of the field.

Another obstacle that early captains quickly overcame was maintaining the integrity of the bait. A rigged mullet, the popular bait of its day, came apart too easily when attacked by a sail. The answer to this dilemma was the use of belly strips cut from small tunas. These strips were discovered to be tough enough to withstand repeated attacks, while maintaining the sail's interest until the fish could be hooked.

With each small development, the sport took on new dimensions. Sailfish soon became a common sight on the docks of South Florida and around the world. As time passed, more and more boats were out in pursuit of sails and other gamefish, and as the times changed, boats and tackle adapted accordingly. Soon, the standard practice of trolling two flatlines simply wasn't enough.

In the late 1920s, fishing legend Tommy Gifford borrowed the idea of suspending baits under a kite. South Pacific fishermen already used this technique, but it was Gifford who brought the idea to Florida. Later, in the 1930s, Gifford would also be credited with development of the modern outrigger, which proved to be a better method to give slack line to a fish after it struck the bait. The dropback of slack line from the outrigger is still essential to today's fishing techniques. The sport really took off after the advent of kites and advanced outriggers.

## Classic Boats

As more people came to vacation in the Sunshine State, more boats got in on the act. Boats that once ran bootleg liquor into Florida from The Bahamas or Cuba suddenly found their owners out of business in 1933, with the

mon catch. The standard procedure was to get out to the dropoff in front of the inlet and then troll along the frequently present rips. There was no need of straying too far from home.

Another reason for staying close to port was the fact that boats of the time were slow, single-engine inboard vessels that were impractical for long-distance runs. Eventually, however, our constant need to go faster and farther took over, and the first twin-engine fishing boats were built.

These new boats allowed the captain to expand his range. It shortened running time to nearby spots, as well as increasing the amount of time on the water actually fishing, instead of just running. In the early 1940s, when these boats really made their appearance, having that ability to run an extra five or 10 miles from the rest of the fleet could mean the difference between 10 sails and 50 on a good day. This big increase in catch over a small distance illustrates how, even in the early days of the sport, fish respond to fishing pressure. Sailfish a few miles from the main fleet were often much more apt to jump on a passing bait.

During the next two decades, boat builders made remarkable strides in their layout and designs. Two families in particular were at the head of the pack in Florida, building what I consider the classic boats in both appearance and function to date. It was Rybovich and Merritt

Modern vessels sprint offshore. Of course, they cost more than the early boats.

repeal of Prohibition. This only added more boats to the charter business. With all these boats out on the water, catch numbers grew by the season.

Before long, 10 to 20 sails a day was a com-

that were on the cutting edge. Rybovich boats were consistently ahead of their time, and are credited with being the first boats to feature the pedestal fighting chair, the gin pole, later the transom tuna door, aluminum outriggers

*Miss Chevy IV* out of Palm Beach was fast for the time and had an early tuna tower that offered no shelter whatsoever. Those early aluminum outriggers were nice but massive compared with today's equipment.

and tuna tower, and a below-deck fish box and livewell, to name only a few innovations.

In 1947, the Rybovich yard completed *Miss Chevy II*, the first sportfishing boat to top 20 knots. That boat would still feel right at home today in any modern marina. This same boat would by my choice of boats to take back in time. A gleaming new 40-knot Jim Smith or Monterey would probably be met by a terrified, torch-carrying mob, and might not get away

Early Rybovich boat, hooked up. The big flag meant a fish was on and to stay clear. Deck space was limited by today's standards.

from the dock before the Navy was dissecting it. (Think of all the new patents, too.)

Roy Merritt and family developed the classic 37 Merritt day boat that danced like a ballerina when battling sailfish off Florida and giant bluefin tuna off The Bahamas at Cat Cay. There are many 37 Merritts still plying the waters off Florida and even Hawaii and St. Thomas. Their lasting popularity is a tribute to their quality and fishability that is undiminished even today.

## Better Tackle and Advanced Electronics

Tackle also was improving and, as today, was changing with the times. Rods went from bamboo to solid fiberglass to tubular glass, while reels became smaller and lighter with more sophisticated braking systems. The old woven, linen lines, prone to rotting if not stripped and dried off the spool, were replaced with nylon, Dacron and eventually synthetic monofilament lines. With more and more people entering the scene, all of these developments were necessary to successfully compete.

Increased fishing pressure, combined with limited resources, meant you had to have the edge over the other guy in order to catch as many fish as in the old days. In the 1960s, that edge would come in the form of electronics: the radiotelephone and depth recorder. You could no longer just "go out front and put the baits out." You had to know where you were in terms of depth. Captains back then were already working together on the radio. Also, taking a land range or "mark" on the beach was a useful way to record your location. By combining water depth with your mark, you could return to a given spot at any time, provided someone didn't cut down the tree you were using for part of your bearing. (That was an early sign of land developers having an effect on fishing.)

When I first started out fishing offshore, sophisticated navigation tools such as your wristwatch and compass would bring you back to a favorite bank or ledge. I even remember one guy, a longliner from Miami, telling me how he kept a record of where he set his gear by taking a heading of about 90 degrees, and watching the depthfinder (which only read to 100 feet or so). When the bottom dropped off, he lit a cigarette and measured his running time by that. Apparently his cigarette consumption was at a fairly measured rate.

This method would be considered extremely low-tech these days. Even a wristwatch would have been more accurate. Seat-of-the-pants navigation was eventually made easier with the development of LORAN receivers. This equipment took modern sportfishing boats to new heights. They were now armed with the ability to see below the vessel, and know not only how deep they were fishing, but to mark fish in the water column and return to the same location repeatedly.

Still, this was only filling the needs of the day, and was necessary equipment to stay competitive. Through the 1970s, modern sport boats became larger, twin diesels were the norm for power, and each boat was equipped with a full assortment of the latest electronics including LORAN, radar, VHF radio, a re-circulating livewell and an array of lever-drag reels on custom wrapped rods.

Finally, the 1980s had us screaming around in 40-knot, air-conditioned 60-footers that are more comfortable to live on than an upscale hotel suite. These boats had color video fishfinders to record plankton and the difference in density between water of varying temperatures; satellite equipment to navigate to within 100 feet of anywhere on the planet; cockpit bait freezers, refrigerated fish boxes, and bag after bag of multi-colored toys to drag behind the boat that splash and spin, rattle, flash, smell and bark like a dog, so to speak.

The 1990s brought on the go-fast, kingfish-style, tricked-out center consoles, many of

**Old Charlie Thompson would roll over in his grave, if he saw the stuff we throw at fish these days.**

Plenty of deck space and fishing room in a fast, center console boat, compared with the old days.

which now push 40 feet in length, powered by three big outboard engines. They have outriggers and big livewells for kite fishing. Some are also capable of 70 knots.

All this to catch the same fish that we were throwing spears at 100 years ago. Old Charlie Thompson would probably roll over in his grave if he saw some of the stuff we throw at fish these days.

## Today's Choices

The trick now is to combine traditional elements of the sport with useful technology available today, and throw out the rest. The hard part may be determining which is useful and which is not. What you'll read from this point on can only be considered my opinion, based on personal experience, and isn't carved on a rock somewhere for future generations.

What you're getting is just information that has helped me to consistently score among the top boats in my field. I've always found there are people who resist changes in this sport, while others embrace every new gizmo on the market like some secret weapon they have to possess, before anyone else gets one. In the middle are those always looking for ways to improve, but usually approach miracle baits and snake oil with skepticism. In fact, most useful new products are developed to meet a need already established by successful fishermen of the day.

I try to remain in the middle group and have found this to be the most productive stance to carry to the offshore rip. With all the progress we've made in the past century, great things are possible any day you spend out there. If you can combine the right elements of the scientific with the artistic, and maintain a sportsmanlike demeanor, you're there. If you can keep those things in perspective, the rest is easy. When someone tells me things aren't like they used to be, I know it's true. But if we stay out on the edge and work at it, using what the past has taught with technology now available, those 15 or 20 sailfish days can still happen.

When they do, we always look back to a bygone era and think, "If I could have one wish..." **SB**

Modern angler and equipment fight the very same sailfish first encountered a century ago. The encounter is just as exciting today.

Early pictures of sailfish jumping were fairly rare; black and white film was slow by today's standards. That made it difficult to freeze-frame those thrashing leaps.

# CHAPTER 4

# Getting the Ride Down

Fishermen have been catching sailfish for many years, perhaps even from primitive craft. Today's anglers use everything from expensive 70-foot battlewagons down to kayaks, to chase these fish. The advantage obviously goes to bigger craft with tall lookout towers with their improved visibility, multiple livewells and air-conditioned comfort.

Other craft score as well: Modern center consoles with their crews have racked up scores of 30 sailfish on that perfect day offshore. These vessels certainly arrive on the spot more quickly, when the weather cooperates. As for kayaks, catching sailfish requires patience and muscle power, while sitting down at water level. It probably requires aspirin by day's end.

**Here's a list of a few items you'll need to take the fight to sailfish, regardless of what kind of boat used. Everything from hooks to safety equipment.**

See DVD for more on prepping your boat.

Today's modern center consoles have room and efficiency to track down sailfish.
This crew is picking up their marker, after fishing a wreck.

# The Sailfish Boat—Your Ride to the Rip

You'll see all manner of watercraft searching for sailfish. Whether you're a casual angler or a die-hard fanatic on a 17-foot center console or a 70-foot battlewagon, there are a few basic items you really should have on the boat to make life easier and increase your success.

## Shade

Shade on an offshore fishing machine is a must. The benefits of a good top are numerous. For one thing, most areas where you chase sailfish are fairly tropical and the sun can be merciless. Obviously, you can last a lot longer on the water if you have somewhere to get out of the sun and you'll stay more comfortable, as well as sharper over the course of a long day. Shade can also be especially helpful from a visibility standpoint, since a lack of glare makes it easier to see into the water and detect fish lurking in your spread before they bite. The extra time you gain to get to the appropriate rod before the line comes tight often makes the difference between a missed and hooked fish. More importantly, a top of some sort affords you the ability to mount outriggers, extra rod holders, an overhead electronics box, even an elevated platform to get above the water for increased visibility. Tops come in all shapes and configurations. Whether it's a T-top, a half-tower or a full-blown tower, a shade top of some sort is a definite improvement to any offshore rig. Of course, summer thunderstorms or raging cold fronts during the winter sailfish run in South Florida make any shelter desirable, especially with clear plastic Isinglass buttoned down from three sides of your t-top.

## Outriggers

In areas where livebait fishing and especially kite fishing are popular, you often see boats set up without outriggers. A lot of livebait special-

Deploying the outriggers by the dawn's early light. This big center console boat has numerous rod holders utilized for trolling, kites and livebait rods.

ists prefer the clean, 360-degree walk-around simplicity of a boat without outriggers, but for maximum versatility—choosing trolling or live-baiting based on the conditions—consider installing outriggers on your sailfish boat.

Some days you just need to cover more water than a dead boat drift allows, and on days like this a pair of 'riggers makes it easier for you to deploy a bigger spread of baits, while you search

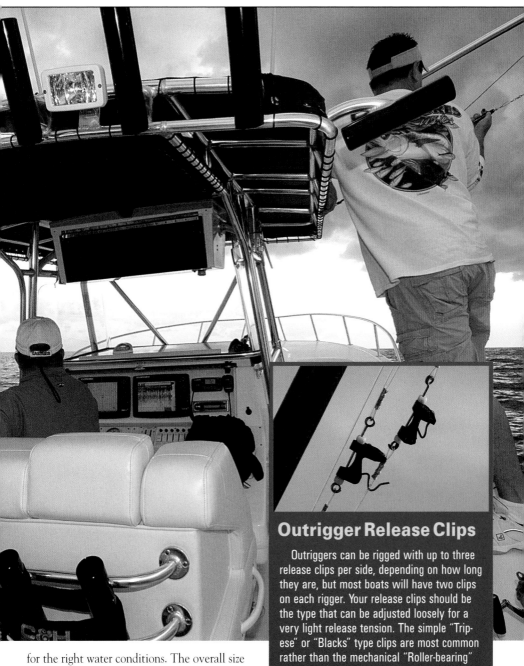

## Outrigger Release Clips

Outriggers can be rigged with up to three release clips per side, depending on how long they are, but most boats will have two clips on each rigger. Your release clips should be the type that can be adjusted loosely for a very light release tension. The simple "Tripese" or "Blacks" type clips are most common rather than the mechanical "Roller-bearing" type. This is important since you should be able to set the tension only heavy enough to keep the line in place and not put any additional strain on the line when a fish grabs the bait. Ultimately, you want the line to fall out of the clip the moment a sail grabs the bait while not alerting the fish, possibly causing it to drop the bait and move on.

for the right water conditions. The overall size of your boat will determine whether you have outriggers from the 15-foot basic models, or full-blown spreader models up to 30 feet long. Spreaders on the longer outriggers make them more stable and stiffer if you happen to be trolling large, heavy baits, but for most sailfish applications your baits won't be heavy enough to place a strain on those 'rigger poles.

# Rod Holders

One item you can never have too many of on an offshore boat is rod holders. Regardless of how many rods you actually deploy, it's always handy to be able to turn around anywhere on the boat and put a rod down in a holder. It has become very popular to line the gunwales with multiple rod holders down both sides of the boat. This configuration is useful for open boats that drift-fish, or fly a kite or two on the downwind side, while various flatlines and deep baits are fished on the upwind side. It's been proven time and again to be well worth the expense of installing as many holders as gunwale space permits, for this type of fishing.

In addition to gunwale-mounted rod holders, many anglers add a "rocket launcher," that allows you to maintain a kite rod and multiple fishing rods from a single location. A rocket launcher is a stanchion-mounted pedestal with several rod holders lined up in a row, that can all be reached from a single location. This makes it easier to simultaneously free-spool the reels and maintain proper distances when kite baits need to be

Watching kite lines, keeping those live baits in the water.

Gearing up for the Miami Billfish Tournament. Sailfish are the primary target here.

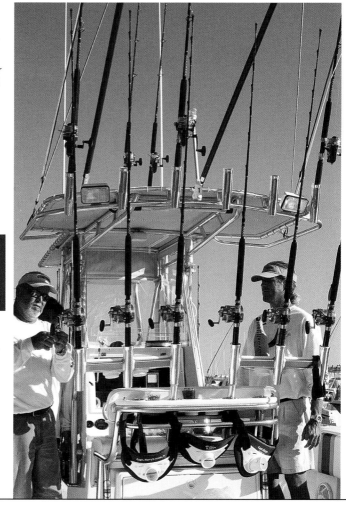

raised or lowered as the wind speed varies. Finally, extra rod holders for storing rods, whether you're running to a spot or simply clearing lines during a battle, are again very useful. They can also be added to your overhead top or tower legs.

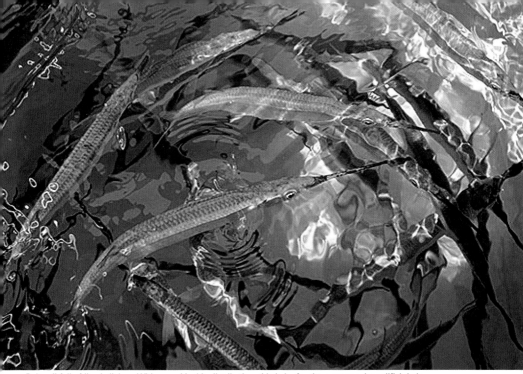

Baitwell full of live ballyhoo. With a world-wide distribution, this is by far the most popular sailfish bait.

## Livewell

Trolling dead bait for sailfish was once the standard technique and considered the most sporting method. Today, more anglers have switched to using live bait. While the debate rages over which method is better, it seems like many more boats will opt for live-baiting if given the choice. The reality is this: If you fish for sailfish in an area where there are a bunch of boats using live bait already, and you want to get in the game, invariably you'll want to use live bait at some point.

In order to do so, you will have to have some type of livewell to carry those baits. Many boats come rigged with factory-installed or built-in livewells. If your boat doesn't have one already, a well can easily be added by simply rigging a saltwater wash-down system and running a hose from this pump to a portable, plastic tank on deck. The water fills the tank and a drain hose at the top of the tank is allowed to run overboard or into a scupper. The tank should be round or oblong without any corners, anything that would prevent baits from swimming freely in circles.

Baits that keep moving in the well stay frisky longer and don't get scuffed up as badly. This makes a much more attractive offering, when you put them back into your spread.

There's simply no need to mix live bait species. Just use two or more livewells. Some boats have four.

The livewell should be large enough to accommodate all the baits you might need, without crowding them. Sufficient water flow should provide enough volume to change the water in the tank constantly. A 500-gallon per hour pump would be considered minimum for providing your baits with a healthy environment. Another minimum rule-of-thumb for tank capacity is that you need at least one gallon of water for every large bait (goggle-eye, blue runner), or for every two smaller baits (sardine, greenie and pilchard) you intend to carry. More volume than this is better if your space allows.

If you have a built-in livewell rigged with its own pump, a wash-down hose is still a welcome addition to your boat. These pumps are handy for cleaning up your work area after a flurry of fish activity. They also make the day's end cleanup much easier—by not allowing blood or fish slime to dry on your decks. This pump can also be used as a backup, in the event your dedicated bait pump breaks down, possibly saving you a day of fishing and even lots of cash, if you purchased your bait. A tank full of happy goggle-eyes isn't cheap.

## Fish Box/Bait Cooler

Although you probably won't need a fish box for carrying home sailfish, you are certain to encounter other kinds of edible fish that are welcome passengers for the ride home. Count wahoo, tuna, dolphin and kingfish among them. It makes good sense to have adequate storage to preserve the freshness of your catch, if a seafood dinner is planned. A fish box should be large enough to accommodate the average sportfish commonly caught around your homeport. It should be well insulated to keep ice from melting, too, keeping in mind that some below-deck fish compartments are sometimes without insulation. In summer heat, they certainly melt ice at a faster rate.

Generally, a 170-quart cooler will more than handle the aver-

age requirement here. You may even have proper fish boxes below deck on your rig, which saves deck space and working room. If space is a concern on your boat, you might also consider an insulated fish bag. These bags are handy since they can be rolled up and stowed away until you need them. You'll still need a smaller cooler to carry ice to put in the bag. As for the bag, on days where no eating fish come aboard, they're out of the way and allow much more room to move around on deck.

If you plan on trolling dead bait, you will certainly need to carry a small bait cooler. A 50-quart cooler is standard for holding trolling baits. Ice should fill the bottom, while leaving enough space inside for all of your rigs and spare bait. A grate between the top of the ice and the baits is placed in the box, to keep baits off the ice and out of the water, as the ice gradually melts. Keeping the fresh baits out of the water will prevent them from "washing out" before you even put them back into your spread. If you decide to fish with natural dredges made up of mullet or ballyhoo, a slightly larger cooler is probably necessary. You may want an additional box just for your pre-rigged teasers.

Pre-rigged ballyhoo baits ready to rock and roll. They're kept above the ice and water, and sprinkled with salt so they won't soften.

Waiting for the strike. Notice three baitwells filled with live bait. Tools and tackle are within a moment's reach.

Keeping hooks dry and handy is the key. You don't want them to rust, especially those that were hand-sharpened and have lost their coating.

## Tackle Storage

Divide your tackle into separate groups. Things that you use constantly throughout the day should be readily accessible at arm's reach. Hooks and terminal tackle items fall into this category and should be stored in watertight plastic containers, which can be left out on a rigging surface, or in a tackle bag. Other items which you won't constantly need to put your hands on, but will probably need before the day is over—such as spare line, lead or leader material—can be stowed away in tackle drawers if you have them, or some type of out-of-the-way storage compartment.

Tackle you bought but never seem to use should be left at home for your next yard sale, since it only clutters up the boat and gets in your way. This leaves room for all of your must-have items. Having extra space on the boat always makes it easier to find things you really need in a hurry.

## Teaser Reels

The boat's top and outriggers also make it possible to add a crucial item to your arsenal. Adding a teaser reel or two allows you to deploy any number of teaser configurations. Considered standard issue on most "high-liner" (high-scoring) boats, teasers raise the ante to a much higher level while chasing sailfish. Running a set of teasers adds a dimension to your spread and gives the appearance of large schools of baitfish swimming along with your boat.

Teaser reels can be as simple as a couple of 4/0 reels clamped to the overhead braces on your top, or a larger single, hand cranked teaser spool rigged with two lines. Many larger

---

**Adding a teaser or two allows you to deploy any number of teaser configurations.**

---

boats opt for more elaborate electric reels, which make it easier to retrieve large, heavy dredge teasers commonly used for tournament sailfishing. All of these reels are rigged with heavy mono or Dacron line testing up to 300 pounds and the lines are sent through a glass eye on the aft corners of your top and finally out to the first guide on your outriggers. A large snap-swivel is attached to the end of the line, to which your teaser of choice is fastened.

## << Electronics Box

An open boat rigged with an overhead top should have a box to house your electronics. Although the popular trend is to flush-mount electronics on your console these days, on smaller open boats the visibility of today's LCD displays is still made more difficult when viewed in direct sunlight. Mounting your electronics overhead in a watertight box makes seeing them when the sun is behind you much simpler and keeps the salt water and spray away from the face of the units as well. An overhead box is also useful for storing other items you need to keep dry, but want easy access to—such as cell phones, cameras or a logbook and pencil to jot notes down in. They also lock up tight when not in use. **SB**

# Safety Equipment

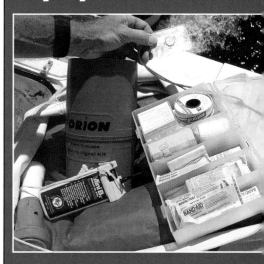

Not really fishing related, but as important as any piece of gear you carry offshore, is adequate safety equipment. Any day you venture offshore on any boat, you face the possibility of some real drama. Being prepared for the worst is always the best policy. The U.S. Coast Guard requires you to have certain safety equipment by law, of course. Life jackets, throwable life cushions, sound signals, fire extinguishers and signal flares are required gear for almost all boats. It never hurts to be over-prepared for a potential emergency, however. Having the best safety gear you can buy is money well spent. Consider adding a 406 MHz EPIRB and a "ditch bag" to your equipment in case of the unfortunate event where you end up in the drink someday.

The EPIRB locator device is encoded with a signal to alert authorities when you're in peril. It has an ID signal unique to your vessel, which transmits your location, thus enabling rescue personnel to locate you more efficiently. A ditch bag is a watertight bag to carry practical items you might need in the event you find yourself on the wrong end of the boat. Fresh water, non-perishable food items, flares and signal lights, your cell phone and more can go in the bag. Simple things like this can make your chances of survival much greater. SB

# CHAPTER 5

# Tackle and Accessories

**Y**ou now have a properly rigged offshore sail-fish machine and need to outfit your boat with all necessary tackle to get down to business. Where to begin? A trip to your local tackle outfitter can be mind-boggling. Shelves are often lined with so many items that it looks like you'll need to take out a second mortgage just to get out the door. Fortunately, to catch sailfish, you don't need to clean out your wallet or tell Junior he won't be going to college. Other than simple terminal tackle and your rods, much of what you see is unnecessary gadgetry. Your initial investment might be fairly substantial and if you have your own boat, you're already aware of this. Once you get started, you'll only need to add inexpensive basic items periodically, to keep the ball rolling. Armed with these items, you'll have all you need for a good day on the water.

**Sailfishing has perhaps more innovations and specialized gear than any other sport.**

Various tools of the trade. Above, helium balloon used to support a kite that will dangle live baits far from the boat on a calm day. At right, different reels for different jobs. Electric reel with short rod at far right retrieves the kite very quickly, once the action begins.

# Sailfish Rods and Reels

The most obvious starting point is your rods and reels. Anglers have a tendency to collect fishing outfits like hunters collect guns. You may have personal favorite rods for certain applications, of course. Depending on your skill level, you may prefer light tackle rather than heavier gear. For sailfish, your spread of rods can be as elaborate or as basic as you like. As a starting point, you'll need a selection that will cover most situations. In a typical application, a selection of six rods would be a good place to begin. You won't have many days where you need more than this: Often enough, four baits in the water and two rods on standby for pitching live baits will suffice.

Standard tackle for sailfish will be a mixture of conventional, lever-drag reels. These should be combined with spin tackle for casting baits at fish sighted in your bait spread astern. Twelve-pound tackle and line would be the lighter end of the spectrum here, with 30-pound on the upper end. Most anglers end up with gear somewhere in the middle. Twenty-pound is ideal, since it's sporting enough to allow you to enjoy the fight, while being heavy enough to whip a fish if you need to put extra heat on him. (Very popular with the tournament crowd, by the way.)

## Four baits in the water and two rods on standby will suffice.

Beautiful set of matched outfits rigged and ready for kite fishing. Styrofoam corks stay 10-15 feet above the water, as visual markers.

See DVD for more on rods and reels.

Kite climbs away into the sky, aided by helium balloon. Large-capacity spin tackle has green neon markers that easily mark each live bait on the surface, often far away.

# Standup Sails

Standup rods with a fast taper and light-action tip are ideal. Fast-taper rods are heavier in the butt section and provide backbone for lifting, while the lighter tip is more sensitive and will enable you to feel the bites better and help you understand what's happening at the business end while you feed a fish.

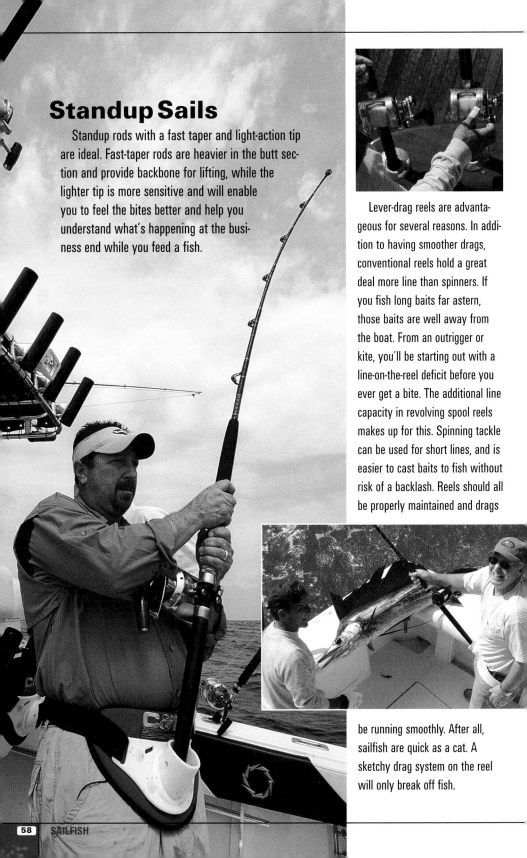

Lever-drag reels are advantageous for several reasons. In addition to having smoother drags, conventional reels hold a great deal more line than spinners. If you fish long baits far astern, those baits are well away from the boat. From an outrigger or kite, you'll be starting out with a line-on-the-reel deficit before you ever get a bite. The additional line capacity in revolving spool reels makes up for this. Spinning tackle can be used for short lines, and is easier to cast baits to fish without risk of a backlash. Reels should all be properly maintained and drags be running smoothly. After all, sailfish are quick as a cat. A sketchy drag system on the reel will only break off fish.

# Clean up Your Tackle

There is no substitute for fine, quality tackle and it is essential when tournament fishing. Maintaining that equipment is also vitally important, no matter how high their quality. These anglers are washing and gently drying their sailfish gear after a day of salty action and spray in the Atlantic during the Miami Billfish Tournament. You can bet they have real confidence in gear like this, when that next fish strikes and makes a lightning-fast run against the drag.

# Line and Leaders

This is another area where personal preference comes into play. There are so many brands of quality line on the market in so many colors, it's hard to decide what to use until you try a few of them out. As for colors, since you normally have a fairly long length of leader at the terminal end, the color of your mainline may have no deterrent effect on fish. Many anglers now favor a high-visibility line on their reels, since it makes tracking the location of each bait much easier. This means a reduced likelihood of crossed lines during turns or while fighting multiple fish,

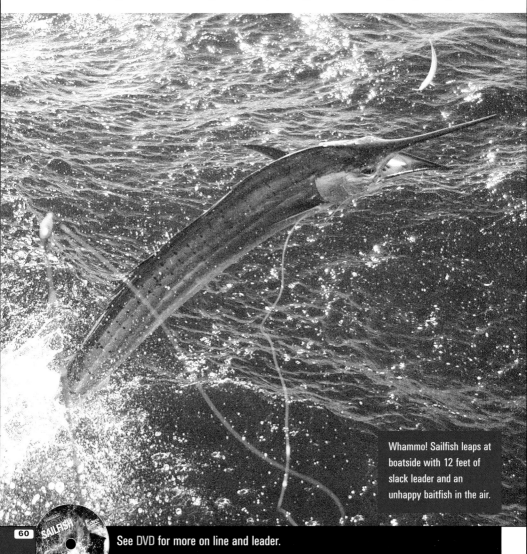

Whammo! Sailfish leaps at boatside with 12 feet of slack leader and an unhappy baitfish in the air.

See DVD for more on line and leader.

and that's certainly a big plus. Regardless of which brand you go with, line should always be changed regularly. The everyday wear-and-tear on fishing line between salt water, floating objects and the sun will eventually cause a failure. That line should be considered the least expensive part of a trip and there's no reason to lose fish after saving a few bucks, not when you consider how much is invested in getting out to the fish. Sailfish tournament crews change their lines each night, after a hectic day offshore. Even if everyone is exhausted, they'll change the lines on 10 reels.

Leader material requires a bit more thought. Since this is the connection between you and the fish's mouth, it becomes important to choose leader that is the least visible. Leaders should still be strong enough to withstand the duration of a battle without fraying through or breaking. Sailfish will sometimes eat baits with reckless abandon and heavy leader or not, they're going to eat. More often though, and especially when they're pressured from other boats, sailfish can become more selective. On such days, it's a sure bet that sharp boat crews will be scaling down their leader size to induce more strikes. Heavy leader for sailfish would be 80-pound test monofilament or No. 7 singlestrand wire. While these leaders will draw strikes from fish that have not been overly pressured, the lighter you make the leader, the more bites. Light or what we call "shy" leader can be as light as 30-pound, but bear in mind you will certainly chafe off more fish while using it. A good selection of mono and fluorocarbon from 30- to 80-pound test and singlestrand wire ranging from No. 4 to No. 7 should be available at all times.

![PRO TIP]

# Pre-rig Leaders

One of the key factors that will lead to a smooth-running billfish program is being completely prepared. Part of any sharp crew's game plan is having what you need right now at your fingertips. This includes (among other things) ready-made rigs to replace the one you just caught a fish on. If you're trolling dead baits, this would involve having an adequate supply already rigged in a cooler, ready to go. For live-baiters, you usually just cut away the rough section at the end of your wind-on leader and tie on a new hook. There are some days, however, when the bite is so fast and furious, you never expect it. Whether it's sailfish bites or others such as bonito or toothy critters, some days you just find yourself out of rigs. This can be costly, when other boats around you are jumping sailfish. Avoid this situation by always having a selection of wind-on livebait leaders with hooks tied on and trolling leaders stored away for just such an emergency. Tie up your leaders at the dock and store in Ziploc bags in bundles of twelve. Add a few shakes of talcum powder to keep moisture out of the bag. To store leaders with fewer tangles, don't tie a loop at the leader's end. The knot forming the loop at the end of a leader is largely responsible for most tangles. Hang all of the hooks, hanging evenly by the leader and wrap all of the lines into a bundled loop together. Secure the leaders together with a piece of copper wire wrapped several times around the loop. SB

# Terminal Tackle and Various Hardware

Having a complete assortment of various hooks and swivels stored in waterproof containers or a dry tackle center is advisable. There are numerous sizes and styles of hooks used for sailfishing. Whether you troll or live-bait with large baits or small, keep a range of tackle on board for both.

You will need different styles of hooks for trolling and livebait fishing. For trolling, the two most commonly used styles are a short-shank hook for rigging small or "dink" bally-hoo, and a standard-shank hook with a "tuna

Sailfisher's tacklebox. Different hooks for those six or eight favorite sailfish bait species, including fresh ballyhoo at far right. Quality swivels and cutting pliers are a must.

See DVD for more on terminal tackle.

bend" for larger ballyhoo, mullet and strip-baits. A tuna hook's point curves in toward the shank and is commonly thought to increase hookups, as well as keeping you connected to a fish once you have him on.

Popular shortshank hooks include the Mustad 9174 or 9175 and the Matzuo 130014. These hooks are both similar designs, with the main difference being the material they're built from. The Mustad versions are not pre-sharpened out of the box and must be touched up with a file before use. The Matzuo is made from pre-sharpened, black chrome plated steel,

which is very handy to have. Why? You don't have as many rusty hook issues, they cost only a few cents more per hook—and that sharp hook is ready to go fishing right now. The Mustad 7766 Tarpon hook is probably the most popular style in the longer-shank style used for rigging larger baits. A good selection of each of these, ranging in sizes from 5/0 to 8/0, should be on board for any occasion.

For live-baiting, the standard is using pricier, pre-sharpened hooks—both traditional J-hooks and circle hooks. These are both available with a chrome finish and sharp right out of the box.

Sweet delicacy for sailfish, a live pilchard with circle hook.

Rigging needles and floss rigging wrap for tying up dead baits and bridling live baits can be stored in their own utility box, as can copper wire for rigging dead ballyhoo. Add a file to sharpen hooks with. Also a felt marker pen, to color over the filed hook points (newly exposed steel) and prevent them from rusting quickly in your tackle box.

Care to land this fish? Invest in premium hooks, for starters. Some of today's brands offer incredible sharpness and durability.

# Hooks

Most sailfish anglers have long realized that, by day's end, those extra hookups are more than worth the extra expense of using premium hooks. Mustad, Owner and others make hooks that fit this description. Owner SSW all-purpose bait hooks, for instance, come in either a super needle point or a slightly more costly but deadly effective cutting point. Mustad offers the Ultra-Point "big gun" livebait hook. All of these hooks are extremely effective for live-baiting sailfish. If you choose to fish with J-hooks, keep a variety in sizes 4/0 to 7/0. For circle hooks, Owner Super Mutu, Eagle Claw circle 2004-Elf Laser Sharp, and Gamakatsu Octopus circles are all popular with the sailfish crowd in sizes 5/0-7/0.

### With this sport, you don't buy a box of 100 dull hooks and go fish.

## Snap Swivels

Quality ball-bearing swivels (both snap type and barrel) come in different sizes and can be stored along with your hooks. For trolling or kite fishing, use snap swivels to prevent line twist. Barrel swivels are handy for a number of rigging applications.

### Mustad 7766
Tarpon 5/0 to 8/0.
Rigging ballyhoo, strip baits or small mullet.

### Mustad
10829 BLN 4/0 to 7/0 ULTRA-Point. All purpose live bait hook.

### Owner
SSW 7/0, black chrome finish. All purpose live bait hook, pre-sharpened.

### Mustad
4/0 to 7/0 live bait hook, model 9174. Economy live bait or trolling small 'hoos or strips.

### Daiichi
5/0 to 7/0 D85Z circle wide bleeding bait hook. Live bait hook, pre-sharpened.

### Matzuo
130014 Rigging trolling 'hoos and strips. With lead after market, for swimming bait.

# Circle Hooks

If you decide to use circle hooks, consider using the style that does **not** have an offset bend, to prevent gut-hooking fish whenever possible. The hook should lay perfectly flat on a table. A common misconception among circle hook anglers is that it isn't possible to gut-hook a fish when using circle hooks. This simply isn't the case and it seems like people are more likely to "feed" or drop back a bait for a longer period while using circles, since they aren't supposed to hook a fish in the throat like a J-hook can. The reality is that many fish, which are originally hooked in the throat, end up having the hook pulled out of their throat and re-hooked in the jaw as the hook slides out of their mouth. This is true of both circle and J-style hooks. That being the case, you should feed a fish a hook for the same amount of time, regardless which style of hook.

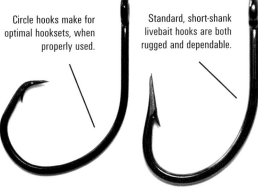

Circle hooks make for optimal hooksets, when properly used.

Standard, short-shank livebait hooks are both rugged and dependable.

---

> **PRO TIP**

## Look Sharp

There are so many choices of hooks these days that are factory sharpened, you might wonder why anyone would use anything else. Whether the cost is an issue, or the fact that not every style is available pre-sharpened, you'll probably find yourself with a file in hand sooner or later. Sharpening hooks with a file is the most effective technique for putting a razor finish on them—but it can get messy. Hook files also remove the coating on a new hook, making them far more prone to rusting. To avoid both the mess of rust filings on your deck and the waste of a box of hooks rusting before their time, try this:

Pre-sharpen a whole box of hooks in one sitting at home for future use. By sharpening them off the boat, you'll avoid the filings rusting on your deck. By doing an entire box you'll always have a sharp hook within arm's reach when you need it. After putting the edge on each hook, use a permanent felt marker to color over the area that has been scratched with the file. This will protect the hook from rusting and when stored in a watertight box, the hooks should keep indefinitely. You can touch up the points that go in the water once you use them, to prolong their effective life as well. **SB**

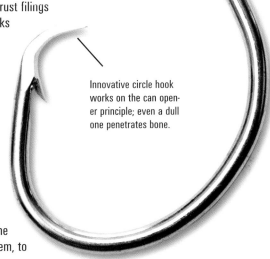

Innovative circle hook works on the can opener principle; even a dull one penetrates bone.

# Bait Catchers

A good selection of various bait-catching rigs, such as sabiki rigs and quill rigs should be on hand, if you intend to catch your own live baits. It always pays to have more sabiki packs on board than you might need, because they are easily tangled from twisting, turning baitfish that are hooked up. These fragile rigs are also prone to attack from various toothy critters like barracuda, that can't seem to resist a string of hooked baitfish.

# Sailfish Lures and Teasers

If you're rigging dead baits for trolling, plan on having days where frozen dead ballyhoo are not holding up under sea conditions. Adding some type of accessory in front of a rigged dead ballyhoo will prevent them from washing out as quickly. They also provide another shot at missed fish that pull the bait apart, rather than pulling only the head and hook away from them. The lure adds dimension and may draw a second bite. While savvy offshore crews often prefer pulling "naked" ballyhoo under ideal conditions, a selection of "sea witches" and small skirts or lures to dress up sub-par baits should be kept on hand, just in case.

A crucial tackle item that can't be left out of your arsenal is a selection of various teasers. It has become more popular over the last few years to rig elaborate teaser spreads and incorporate them into a trolling program. A better way to describe it might be to incorporate baits into your teasers, since the teasers of choice are often multi-bait, schools of fish rigged on spreader bars and umbrella frames. It's conceivable to have up to 100 teaser baits working for you, which can overwhelm your four baits with hooks. This type of teaser is known as a "dredge" and may contain as many as 48 baits on each frame.

**A selection of "sea witches" and small skirts or lures to dress up sub-par baits should be kept on hand.**

When you see lots of natural bait dredges made up of split-tail mullet or ballyhoo around the tournament docks, that's when artificial baits are gaining acceptance. Various soft plastic baits such as swimming shad, ballyhoo and squid can be rigged on these frames and extra baits should be stored

A variety of colored skirts pulled in a big spread willl hopefully entice the pickiest sailfish.

See DVD for more on teasers.

Ballyhoo with colored skirt above plows water behind the boat. Use a variety of skirt colors for best action.

in the event of toothy critter attacks. Also gaining popularity are synthetic plastic strips with reflective baitfish images attached along their length. These are attached to the dredge frame and are highly reflective, as well as easy to store when not in use. Along with your dredges, you'll need to keep several cigar leads on hand to run just ahead of the teaser, to keep it in the water.

In addition to dredge teasers, the old stand-by "daisy chain" teasers still find their way into the spread and are very popular for days when you find yourself short-handed and the dredge teasers are too much work. Daisy chains are also easier to store. Most daisy chains consist of a string of six to 10 baits strung in a line. The most commonly used bait for rigging daisy chains are rubber squids and sailfish really do love them. Regardless of which teaser type you end up with, they're invaluable and should be a part of any sailfish spread.

In addition to dredge teasers, the old stand-by "daisy chain" teasers are very popular.

Artificial dredge imitates a school of baitfish following the boat. Pelagic predators can't help but attack. Below is a dredge made from real mullet, messier and more time-consuming. At far left is the old-fashioned, plastic squid teaser, which still works.

# Kites and Kite Rods

If you plan to kite-fish with live bait, on gelspun poly, you'll need a kite rod and reel—which is a short rod and reel rigged with Dacron line and pre-rigged with swivels and release clips dedicated to flying a kite only. You'll want a selection of kites to match various wind speeds, in addition to the stubby kite rod. There are kites designed for use with wind speeds varying from 10 knots on up to 25 knots. You will need to stock a few different models. One manufacturer of fishing kites also has a model designed to fly in any wind condition and while they may be more expensive, substituting one high-dollar kite for three less expensive may be more practical.

**You will want a selection of kites to match various wind speeds, in addition to the stubby kite rod.**

Electric kite reel above has replaced some of the older Penn reels that were used for many years.

SAILFISH

See DVD for more on kites.

Launching the kite can be tricky, because the wind flow is interrupted by the boat's superstructure. If the wind waffles or stops, the kite may crash and become soggy. That means rinsing in fresh water and then drying, before launching again.

# A Few Things to Remember

Needlenose pliers used for multiple purposes. The plastic tools in neon are safe release knifes, great for cutting leaders when action gets really hectic. Gloves protect hands from rough bill.

**A** set of tools including knives, pliers, and scissors should be at arm's reach. A knife is handy for various rigging applications and to cut a leader when releasing fish. Fishing pliers with side cutters are useful for cutting line and wire as well as removing hooks from fish. A pair of bolt cutters is a smart thing to keep on any boat, in case you find yourself stuck with a hook and need to remove it. Game shears are scissors, sold in sporting good stores. They're used for cleaning game birds, but are popular offshore for cutting

line or light wire. They also cut dead bait or chum; they're a common sight on fishing boats. Two pairs of gloves will also come in handy for grabbing the leader or bill of the fish, before releasing it. Lightweight gloves that won't bind your hands up into a knot are practical. Bring a pair of cotton garden gloves, along with a pair of the popular synthetic gloves with rubber webbing melted over the palms for grip. You won't bill and release many sailfish without gloves; their bills are raspy as a file, very tough on bare hands. **SB**

# Gaffs and Tag Sticks

Although you won't need to gaff a sailfish, you're certain to encounter other gamefish that you'd like to bring home and a gaff should be on hand for landing these fish. Additionally, if you plan on tagging any sailfish you catch, you'll need a tag stick and selection of tags and information cards. These should be stored dry in an easily accessible location, so that you can quickly rig a tag on your stick and not subject the fish to any additional stress at boat-side, while you search around for your tag kit. It's in the Tupperware box, right?

# Sunglasses

Last but not least, one of the most important pieces of equipment you can take to the water is a pair of quality, polarized sunglasses. Going fishing without a pair of good sunshades is just not practical. Polarized lenses eliminate blue light scatter and surface glare, making it possible to peer beneath the surface at baits and fish in your spread—along with other marine life, which may be of interest. The ability to see fish in the water and make a pass with your baits, seeing a fish in your spread before it eats, will account for many bonus catches. Another benefit of wearing quality eyewear is the protection of your own vision from hazardous ultraviolet rays. It makes sense to spend a little extra money for your own personal pair of shades as well as to keep a couple of pairs of inexpensive replacements on the boat. Spare glasses come in handy for days when a guest on your boat doesn't have glasses or if someone drops theirs overboard. A smart idea to save your own quality glasses is to attach a lanyard, so they won't fall overboard when you hang over the gunnel, dealing with a fish. SB

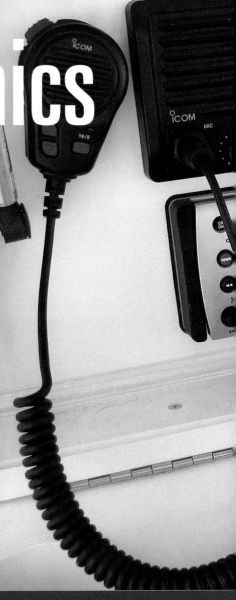

# CHAPTER 6

# Electronics

O nce you've learned the basics about sailfish habits and habitats, you'll want to have the right tools for reading the water. Certain shipboard electronic systems are as vital to the sailfish angler as specialized, diagnostic tools are to physicians and mechanics. Important signs are beneath the surface, such as midwater baitfish schools, dropoffs and thermoclines.

Sonar units, very affordable these days, portray these and other features on compact, console-mounted screens. It's also valuable to know your position, and how to quickly navigate to fishing hotspots. Global Positioning System (GPS) units give you an instant fix, using signals from orbiting satellites. GPS chartplotters accept digital chart cards and may have greater detail than paper charts. VHF radio is also a necessity for boat safety and eavesdropping on the fleet.

## Modern electronics are crucial to so many aspects of fishing offshore.

See DVD for more on electronics and reading the water.

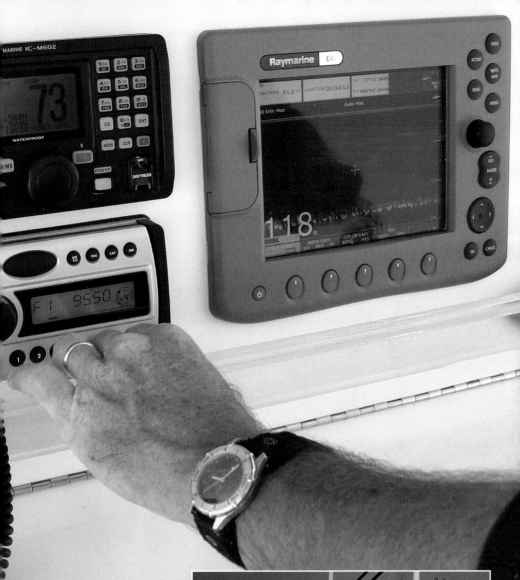

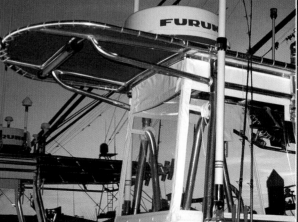

Even the smaller boats won't leave the inlet often without an electronic array, including VHF radio and GPS, just for starters. Newer upgrades constantly arrive each year.

# High-Tech Versus Low

**E**arly on, anglers targeting sailfish on rod and reel were limited to "instinctive" fishing techniques. Lacking the technology we have today, anglers simply went offshore looking for obvious signs of life and started fishing. Birds feeding, baitfish on the surface under stress, visible current edges and even the target species swimming along on the surface were all useful signs that you were in the right neighborhood. It was that simple and with the limited number of competing boats, coupled with a far greater number of fish to chase, high catch rates were fairly common.

Today, an angler has many more boats to contend with and perhaps fewer fish to split up among the fleet. This may seem like a disadvantage at first, but when you consider the modern tools we have at our disposal to find hidden signs, along with the fact we can still see the obvious ones, we are certainly playing way above the heads of old-time anglers.

Modern electronics enable us to move fully and understand what is going on down below. We not only know how deep the water we fish is, but also what the bottom is shaped like, even composed of. We know whether there is fish-attracting structure beneath us and if there are predator fish down below. On top of this, we're able to know exactly where we are within a few feet and return to an identical location day after day, never guessing about anything other than if the fish will bite at that very spot.

It's tough to hide below, when boats above carry the latest electronics, with skippers who know how to use these systems and interpret what they're seeing.

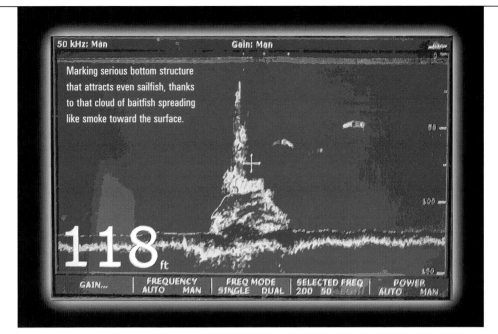

50 kHz: Man       Gain: Man

Marking serious bottom structure that attracts even sailfish, thanks to that cloud of baitfish spreading like smoke toward the surface.

**118** ft

GAIN... | FREQUENCY AUTO MAN | FREQ MODE SINGLE DUAL | SELECTED FREQ 200 50 | POWER AUTO MAN

## Depth Sounder/ Fish Finders

Probably the most obvious use for a depthfinder is its name, finding the depth of the water. Simply knowing how much water is under your boat is basic but critical to fishing. This is really just the tip of the iceberg. If you regard your depthfinder as your eyes below the surface, it opens up a world of possibilities. A depth recorder will draw a picture of the ocean floor for you. Some of today's depthfinders are capable of drawing a three-dimensional map of the bottom, detailing every crack and crevice, while revealing all the sealife between your boat and the ocean floor in vivid colors. While it's understood that most of us don't have that kind of technology on board, you can still use your imagination to create an image of the bottom by looking at a two-dimensional screen while watching depth changes and paying attention to details.

With repeated visits to an area, you will gain familiarity with the depth changes such as sharp dropoffs, reefs and wrecks. By combining this with the knowledge of your location,

Affordability is always important, but try not to skimp on vital electronic equipment that may mean the difference between a great day and a disastrous one. A system for mapping the bottom and surrounding terrain along nearby shorelines is just one handy item introduced by manufacturers. Most skippers would rather forget their boat keys, than leave port without a dashboard of their favorite electronics.

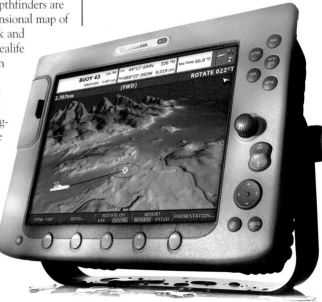

## Your fishfinder will help you find that structure and identify if something is there. It helps determine what type of sealife is below.

you soon start to "see" the bottom in a different light. As you become more familiar with terrain you should start to imagine it as a three-dimensional surface, which it is. Knowledge of what the bottom is shaped like helps you understand how the current relates to the bottom and forms rips and edges, which in turn attract the fish.

With this under your hat, you will better understand why the fish you "mark" on that recorder are probably there. As the machine is drawing the bottom, visualize the ocean floor as its shape relates to the water moving across it. Additionally, you'll recognize the fact that almost all structure will contain some type of life at one time or another. Marine life forms are all subjected to the same daily challenge of trying not to become a food item—from the

smallest life forms to the billfish we're after. By starting at the bottom of the food chain and working your way to the top, you'll notice that all of it relates to some kind of structure when feeding time begins. Your fishfinder will help you find that structure and identify if something is there. It will help determine what type of sealife we are dealing with and ultimately convert this knowledge into a possible bite.

A bronze through-hull transducer with a 50/200 KHz dual frequency transducer will give you better performance than a transom-mount model. Always install it in the proper location where it won't be subjected to a lot of white water or turbulence, which will diminish its performance.

An additional feature found on many transducers is a surface temperature gauge. Whether

# High End Fishfinders

Experts advise adding the highest quality depth recorder to your arsenal that your budget allows. The offshore industry is producing some very sophisticated equipment and at a price affordable to small boaters. As a starting point when considering a bottom machine, you should look for a good quality color LCD display with a minimum of 500 watts output, up to as much as 1,000 watts.

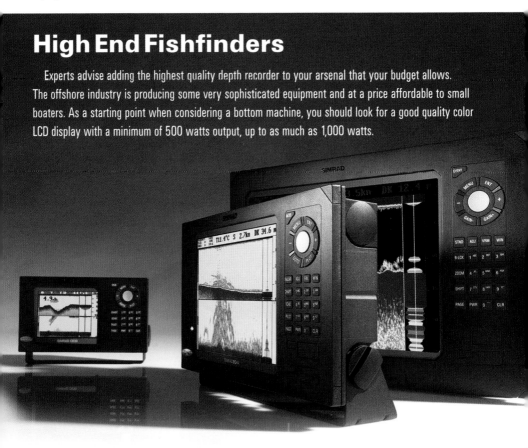

you have one on your bottom machine or a separate stand-alone unit or both, this is a crucial tool for locating action on the sailfish grounds. Sailfish are temperature-sensitive creatures and in areas like the east coast of Florida, temperature may be the most important factor that dictates their movements. Knowledge of any variance or gradient in sea surface temperatures is a key component in locating where these fish move to overnight. Knowing that will help you get back on the fish after a lapse in the action or when the fleet seems to have lost the fish. Locating a "break" in the water temperature is also a useful tool for finding something different to fish over, when more obvious signs like a color change or rip aren't visible to the eye. Regardless of all else we use to catch or find fish, water temperature is the only thing you can't see with your eyes.

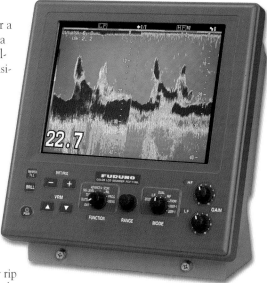

Finally and most importantly, take the time to read your owner's manual and learn to use your machine to its fullest potential. By turning to the automatic settings on everything, you're taking the easy way out. Learning to tune the machine manually is the first step to understanding the finer points of what the equipment can actually do to help you catch more fish.

Water temperature readings are vital, because all fish react to their comfort zone. You wouldn't want to waste your time trolling in 60-degree water for sailfish, for instance. Know your targeted fish species' favorite zone and concentrate efforts there.

## GPS/Chartplotter

Familiarity of the ocean floor is of little use, if you don't know exactly where you are. Combining knowledge of the shape of the bottom with the awareness of your exact location makes it possible for this information to stick and allows you to return to that location anytime you like for a look around. Remember the learning curve? A Global Positioning System, or GPS, will get you back to the same location over and over again.

A GPS unit alone will

Electronics providing more than one function have become quite popular, saving space on the console. This one happens to be plotting your course while approaching home port, while also mapping the bottom below.

show your position in latitude and longitude, as well as a host of other useful navigation data such as speed, heading, time of day and more. It will enable you to navigate directly to a known location such as a wreck or reef or any favorite fishing spot.

A GPS combined with a chartplotter takes you to the next level. The chartplotter will draw a line representing the track of your boat and where it has traveled in a series of dots. This "crumb trail" shows where you've been and is most useful to re-trace your path when

depth reading to circle around on the same spot, you would be all over the place. Try it some time with just your eyes and refer to the plotter after a few minutes and see how well you did. You might be surprised to learn how difficult it is to sit tight over a specific location using only your eyes. In contrast to this approach, by referring to the track line on a plotter, it's possible to cover the exact piece of water over and over again within a few feet. This technique would be especially useful if the bite came on top of a small fixed location such as a rockpile or a wreck holding baitfish.

## Plotters

A plotter is also useful for storing locations where you've had action such as the above described, as well as hazards to navigation, even important points such as inlets or buoys. Another useful function of the plotter is to

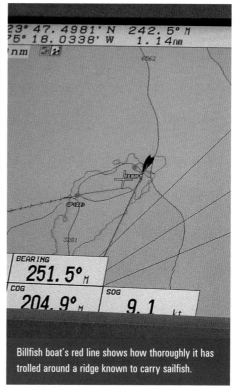

Billfish boat's red line shows how thoroughly it has trolled around a ridge known to carry sailfish.

you drive over something of interest or get a bite. The track line also helps you stay oriented to points on land or other boats, while busy trying to study your depth recorder, or keep on top of some structure down below. Again, like the depth recorder, this requires creative thinking, but it's not as difficult as it sounds.

For example, if you were trolling along and got a bite in 200 feet of water and wanted to turn around and circle over the spot, you might think it's as easy as making a circle and looking at the bottom machine to repeat the same depth. The reality is, if the current is moving you along and the wind is blowing you in a certain direction and you simply relied on your

help accumulate "waypoints" of known hotspots, which you'll no doubt collect over time. As you acquire a collection of these saved locations, patterns begin to emerge. You will save a lot of time (formerly wasted) guessing where to set out. It means gaining the upper hand over other anglers who are simply fishing blind, or following you around. A good rule of thumb for assembling a collection of waypoints is to start out by noting any bottom structure

you find interesting and saving it, including where you got a good bite. You'll soon figure out the two locations will commonly be found together. Pay attention to patterns drawn on your plotter screen, and the waypoint symbols will draw a map of the structure for you, while showing you which areas along the structure

# Secondary Equipment When recreational traffic gets hea

Among the tools you'll find useful for locating the bite, other than the two most important ones above, are a VHF radio and a radar unit. A VHF radio is most useful to communicate with others in the event of an emergency or mechanical breakdown and subsequently, is generally standard equipment on all boats for that purpose.

son alone, having a few friends to network with and share information with can certainly save the day. In addition to your own personal group of friends, you can learn a lot by simply keeping your ears tuned in to the chatter going on among the fleet of boats that you don't know.

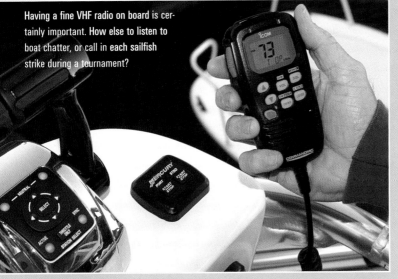

Having a fine VHF radio on board is certainly important. How else to listen to boat chatter, or call in each sailfish strike during a tournament?

Most locations you'll fish have a local channel used by the charter fleet and it's always wise to simply lie in the background and listen to what they are talking about without disturbing them. When the recreational traffic gets heavy on the radio, you'll find the professional captains get a bit more tight-lipped. A fact to consider is no matter how secretive some folks like to be when it comes to how good or bad the fishing is, soon-

Another useful function for a radio is to network with other fishermen and to monitor action taking place on other boats. Networking is important for a number of reasons. Sailfish have a tendency to move around a lot, and the bite will shift as they change locations. Having the ability to listen to other anglers and their daily chatter on the VHF will keep you informed of what's going on over a big geographic area. It's common to experience a mediocre day in one spot, while a few miles away another group of boats are racking up multiple releases just out of your sight. For this rea-

er or later, everyone talks. Some may use their cell phones, but not all. You may not hear specific details and locations being thrown around but somebody in the middle of a hot bite will eventually crack and call someone in to join them. So, the VHF is a valuable component on the boat, besides for safety's sake.

Finally, a radar, though not as useful for fishing in most sailfish locations, can still be very handy. They're more commonly used to navigate in fog, thunderstorms and darkness. Few locals where sailfish prowl actually experience fog, but it hap-

have been productive.

Again, you should buy up to the highest level you can afford for this equipment as well. The added cost is realized not so much in how accurate the device is anymore, but in how functional the features are. And how user-friendly the unit is. If you find it frustrating to go through an elaborate series of keystrokes to perform the simplest task on your GPS, you'll probably stop using it eventually. Buying quality is money well spent. Like the depth recorder, this is a tool difficult to live without, if you're serious about offshore fishing. **SB**

pens. If you do live in a spot that requires boat travel before or after the sun, a radar unit is a true convenience. As a fishing tool (other than for locating flocks of seabirds) the one useful function of radar is in locating a fleet of boats just out of your range of vision. This is often a sign that something is going on that you need to know about. In populated areas along the coast, when a large fleet of boats is busy chasing sailfish, and somebody gets into fish, other boats close in on them. Gradually you may see what appears to be a fairly spread out bunch of boats turn into a tight cluster. While you might not immediately want to run right in and join them, you would at least be aware of the location where a good bite is taking place for later reference. Or you can get in and fish around the outskirts of the crowd until the gold rush mentality settles down. A radar unit combined with your VHF radio can be your eyes and ears in the distance and for this reason they're certainly tools you should consider having on board.

All things considered, having good electronics on your tricked-out sailfish rig will ultimately make you a more productive participant in the sport. That gives you a decided advantage over many boats you'll be sharing the water with, and ultimately means more fish for you. It's wise to really take the time to master this equipment and get it working to its maximum potential. That still doesn't get you any closer to getting your baits in the water. Let's get down to the nuts and bolts of actually fishing for sailfish. **SB**

Radar is now mounted on small and smaller boats, very useful for spotting even diving birds—let alone approaching storms.

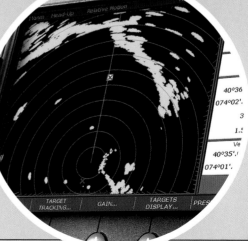

40°36
074°02'.
3
1.5
Ve
40°35'.
074°01'.

TARGET TRACKING...    GAIN...    TARGETS DISPLAY...    PRES

# CHAPTER 7

# Time to Go Fishing

**Y**our boat is rigged with gear, and tackle is in order. You've been waiting all week to get on the water and catch a sailfish. What about a game plan? Many factors will influence how you spend a day offshore—which method to use and where to fish. Decisions have to be made beforehand, such as what bait to use, whether live or dead. Where to fish is also important, a decision usually based on where the fleet was catching fish yesterday, or the day before.

Weather conditions are important and water clarity a big factor. All of this has to be added up before leaving the dock; you certainly don't want to make a simple guess, once the jetties are cleared. Catching a fine day of action on the water does require some homework, but that's part of fishing.

## To have that 10 or even 20 sailfish day, you've got to do your homework.

Center console boat sprints offshore, heading for the latest sailfish bite. These guys are moving like they have a purpose; obviously they've done a little homework and networking before heading out.

# Networking With Anglers

**"Dock talk" means that fishermen are sharing information between trips offshore. Useful tips can be picked up here. Very often, that next trip offshore begins here.**

There are a number of ways to gather information that will get you pointed in the right direction. For starters, you probably have friends who fish offshore. If you've been in the boating game for any length of time, you've surely noticed how most people like to talk about their success (or even failures) on the water. A typical day on the

Knowing which direction to point your boat each morning is one of the keys to success.

water usually ends with some dock talk or phone time, running down the day's events, discussing who did what and where, how many fish were seen or caught by which boats. And what offshore conditions were like. That's all part of how today's fishermen network. Everybody does it, from the casual weekend sport to the professional fishing guide or charter crew. Even commercial fishermen. Talk to as many people as you can before heading offshore, and follow the action on days when you can't be on the water. Keep abreast of water quality, baitfish availability and fish movements. Having recent, first-hand information from people you trust is invaluable. It's also a two-way street, and in the long run it pays to

There is lots of useful information to be found on the docks, before and after each trip. Even the slightest tip can help avoid hours of fishing in the wrong area. Of course, a hot tip is almost priceless, depending on how much you value a great day of action offshore. You have to sift the wheat from the chaff, so to speak.

be generous with your own information and observations out there, as well. Few people will share information freely with someone who never seems to have anything useful to offer back. Making friends on the water and at the dock may not seem easy at first, but after you start putting up some respectable release numbers, you'll be surprised how many folks want to hear what you have to say.

After time spent on the water, many anglers pick a handful of people they share information with and may be reluctant to talk freely with just anyone on the dock. Personal experience has taught me that you can learn something from anybody, however. Taking a minute to talk with someone whom the "experts" won't give the time of day to may lead to useful information. Don't be hesitant to ask questions of anyone. What you do with that information is up to you, but never rule out a chance to listen to someone talking freely on the dock.

Fish talk is not just limited to the local marina, either. There are other people swapping fishing stories on dry land, as well. Talking on the phone with fishing buddies is an obvious option, but don't forget to keep an open line of communication with your local tackle shop. Any port you fish out of will have one or more shops and they generally keep abreast of what has been going on from day to day. While that information may be a little more broad or general than a detailed account from a personal friend who actually fished yesterday, it's a start.

Another source of information is the Internet. Many fishing-related Websites feature updated reports from anglers and charterboats. That can be a handy source of information, found while at home or even the office. Most of what you read on these reports is a daily rundown of who caught what and where, just the type of knowledge you are looking for. To go a step further, you can also find a variety of fishing forums or chat rooms, where anglers go into greater detail about what's been happening on the water. Participants in these discussion groups tend to be a little more free with the information they share. Establishing a presence or (better yet) a reputation on one of these sites will often lead to a better relationship with a number of anglers. These folks tend to be tuned in to what the entire fleet is doing and will discuss more openly what is going on offshore, even on a daily basis. It's also an arena to meet friends who share a common interest.

What type of informa-

Even highly seasoned fishermen can pick up a few clues on the Internet, thanks to today's fishing forums and chat rooms.

Moment of triumph, a happy angler with great big sailfish. This is the end result of networking with other anglers.

tion are we looking for before leaving the dock? Knowing where sailfish were yesterday greatly narrows the playing field. Still, that info gives a cold trail to follow—if we don't consider the reasons why they were there to begin with. A full understanding of the reasons why is critical once we get on the water. A better understanding of reasons why the bite takes place is critical to your success, once you actually put the 'riggers out. Keep in mind that staying in touch with your network of friends on the water while you are actually fishing is

as important as it was before you left the dock. There will, however, come a time where you are on your own—and a solid understanding of where the sailfish want to be and why, is going to be the only thing that puts flags in the 'riggers. To more thoroughly grasp the reason why some boats catch 10 sailfish while other boats catch only one, you have to consider the needs of the fish and exploit them to your advantage. Let's take a look at a sailfish's basic needs and how they relate to us, before we tangle with them. SB

# CHAPTER 8

# The Triangle: Food, Structure, Water Quality

**O**ne might wonder why it is that only a handful of anglers always seem to catch more fish than everybody else. Although it may seem like you're doing everything right, you may never get that little extra edge and come out on top. It's true that 10 percent of anglers catch 90 percent of the fish. If you've wondered why the rest of the group don't cross over into the 10 percent club, consider this—to gain that kind of result you have to understand why you get the bites.

Most anglers seem content to simply know they are using the proper bait and are in an area where the fish hang out. To really understand the whole picture, think about all of the factors, such as when and why these fish are feeding in a given area.

## Three key ingredients for finding the best action on sailfish.

See DVD for more on reading the water.

To have a multi-sailfish day, you have to key in on some basic factors that sailfish are attracted to.

# Sailfish Mysteries

Trying to unravel the mystery of a fish's daily activity can be the most daunting task we face as anglers. It's difficult to say with any certainty what is going on in a sailfish's brain at any given moment. While there are facets of their life we will never

Tournament winning team from Boynton Beach, Florida, hooked up with yet another sailfish.

understand, there are things that we definitely know and can use to our advantage. A predatory animal like the sailfish is driven by some very basic needs: food and comfort. These are the major factors we need to consider, when

trying to locate sailfish.

Finding a plentiful source of protein in water they can tolerate is what drives a sailfish and shapes its daily prowlings. To thrive, sailfish live in a temperature range between 72 and 85 degrees. Although they're found in waters above and below this range, excesses in either direction certainly affect their movement. Temperature shifts on the lower end of the spectrum will influence their movement more notably. Typically, you'll find sails moving south during the cooling months to escape falling water temperatures and north during warming months as temperatures moderate. A classic example of this movement is the fall and winter southerly migration of sailfish we experience on the Atlantic coast of Florida. These fish make their way south as each passing cold front drives water temperatures below their tolerable range. The bite begins for anglers off Northeast Florida in the fall, and moves southward through midwinter until anglers in South Florida and the Keys are catching them through the spring. By summer, the fish are pushing back north and spreading out across the lower half of the eastern seaboard.

The trick is finding them as they pass through your neck of the woods—and offering them something they want. To accomplish this, you need to consider three things and how they relate to one another.

## Water quality

Clean ocean water is a wonderful thing, especially when it collides with greener coastal water, concentrating baitfish and predators.

First and foremost is food. Sailfish won't be found hanging around for any length of time where there isn't food. Reputable hotspots are always adjacent to a healthy supply of forage fish. Finding a number of sailfish passing through an area holding bait is a dream scenario. If the water quality is just right and the food is there, these fish will be reluctant to leave.

The second point to consider is structure, which holds bait. Doing your homework and familiarizing yourself with locations where baitfish congregate is again crucial to your success. Whether it's reefs both artificial and man-made, natural ledges, wrecks or rockpiles, there are always certain structures that bait-fish favor. Spending time becoming familiar with such bait hangouts will get you one step closer to a sailfish bite. Not to mention the added benefit of a ready supply of live bait.

**Finding water of suitable temperature, clarity and current is the third point of the triangle.**

The final part of the equation is water quality. Finding water of suitable temperature, clarity and current is the third point of the triangle. These three things are always tied together. Water current runs across structure and forms edges, which attract bait that ultimately attracts sailfish. Moving water also forces fish to keep swimming, which increases their need for food. That's pretty simple, when you think about it. Finding all three of these elements working together is ideal. While this is not always a reality, it's what we shoot for when trying to establish a location to set out our spread of baits.

Consider these three items in order of importance. Bait may be the most important factor, since sailfish are able to tolerate water that is less than ideal in temperature and clarity, as well as a lack of structure—as long as bait is present. If you could only have one of these elements working in your favor, I would certainly choose a

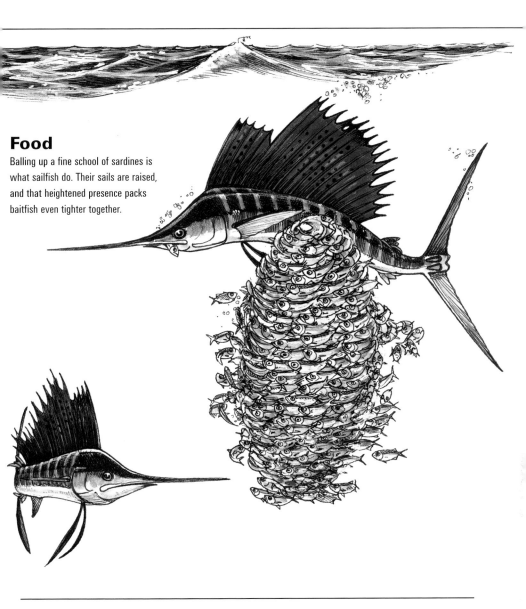

## Food

Balling up a fine school of sardines is what sailfish do. Their sails are raised, and that heightened presence packs baitfish even tighter together.

**Bait may be the most important factor, since sailfish are able to tolerate water that is less than ideal in temperature and clarity.**

ready supply of bait. As it happens, however, you usually won't find one without the other two. When you take a minute to contemplate how the three factors are tied together, it seems like common sense when you try to choose a place to start looking for fish. Bait relates to structure, since it offers baitfish security and a solid structure to orient to and hide around when predators arrive and go on

a feeding frenzy. The water also relates to the structure, creating rips and eddies as it flows past and around the relief. These current breaks concentrate microorganisms, which the baitfish feed on. This in turn attracts larger predators such as sailfish.

So how do we translate this knowledge into creating a plan for finding and catching sailfish? Start by looking at the one constant.

Water will change in terms of quality and the bait will move in and out of the area, but solid structure always stays the same. By combining the knowledge of where the bite has been (through networking) and familiarity of local bottom structure—and using your electronics—you have a big head start.

Once an area of interest is determined, start checking out nearby structure for the other two factors, water quality and bait. If you find them all working together in the same neighborhood where the bite has been, go fishing. That's a pretty basic concept, but it works.

Using this knowledge to help locate productive fishing grounds is what separates the high-liners from the also-rans. Rather than simply walking the "donkey trail" and following the fleet around, it's always more enjoyable to be first boat on the fish. Finding a bunch of sailfish to yourself, before

## Structure

Sunken wrecks and prominent rock ledges attract baitfish balls and sailfish, that will hang around for days if the food supply remains.

**boat to find the fish.**

the fleet piles in, is a nice way to target a high number of fish without dealing with a crowd of boats.

There will be days when all of this thinking is done for you in advance, of course. Being off by yourself is always enjoyable, but when the fleet is in the middle of a "mad dog bite" and everyone has a fish hooked up, well, it's wise to take a number and jump into the

# Tailers

A phenomenon peculiar to sailfish is their habit of tailing in large seas. This is especially common during times when these fish are in a mass migration mode. For example, during a typical winter's cold front in the Gulf Stream, gusty north winds will blow directly against this famous current coming up from the south. These steep swells produce classic tailing conditions, and sailfish love to get on top and ride. Often you will see several fish at a time surfing downhill, heading south for warmer water. A bunch of fish in a row with their tails exposed have actually been compared to a picket fence.

A picket fence of tailing fish isn't just for watching, however. It's easy to get ahead of them and throw baits. Often these fish go unnoticed by novice anglers. The trick to spotting them (the fish) is not to look for a dark-colored, lit-up shadow. When sailfish are in this mode, they swim with all of their fins tucked away and take on a very dull, slate gray color. This coloration makes them blend in with the background so well, they can be completely overlooked. Any day you find swells standing up, you should be looking into the crests of the swell where the light shines through it. This effect will backlight the shadow of a sailfish and makes spotting them easy. Keep an eye peeled away from your spread so you have time to move your baits into position before the fish reach you. Always be ready to sight-cast a pitch bait to them as they pass by. On days where you repeatedly see fish tailing, don't overlook the possibility of just hunting for them with a trolling spread out and getting your boat into position for a frontal assault.

The combination of hunting and fishing can add a fresh element to your experience.

action. Some days, especially in areas with a lot of fishing pressure, you just have to join the crowd. Most days when the action is hot and heavy, other boats will know about it, and a fleet appears out of thin air. It's those days during a lull in the action and everyone's off hunting for action that knowledge of local terrain and bait movement will save the day.

Something to consider when you decide to go off on your own and search for the next bite: Fishermen are certainly creatures of habit, and most people rely on other boats to find fish for them. The old salts still remember

the old days, "When people used to look for fish, not boats." And with good reason. Most boaters today would rather have someone else do the work for them when it comes to finding the sailfish bite. In fact, many people simply stop and set out their baits based on the fact that somebody else is already fishing there. That's getting back on the "donkey trail" again. When considering this fact, it's no surprise that you'll often see the same boats in the same spots day in and day out, regardless of how good or bad the fishing is. Few captains want to be the pioneer. With

limited time on their hands to enjoy fishing, the easiest thing to do is just go to the usual spot and hope for the best. A much bolder move is to take your chances and think outside of the box.

Sailfish do have tails and cover a large area of water over the course of a day. They may be on the beach in 30 feet of water in the morning and out to 600 feet by that very afternoon. These fish are always on the move looking for an ideal situation. If you're fishing in an area without the above described conditions (bait, structure, water quality) and not getting bites, never be afraid to take a chance and go off in a search mode. Remember what the fish needs and go find it. Sailfish, unlike other billfish, can tolerate some extreme conditions. They're as common close to Florida's Atlantic beaches as they are in the Gulf Stream. On days where the action isn't happening on the dropoff, (the common starting point on the east coast of Florida), we just assume the last bunch of fish has passed us by, and wait for the next weather system to send us more. Many intervals of slow fishing have occurred off "Sailfish Alley" while scores of fish fed freely in the non-traditional locations close by and unnoticed.

Assuming you've done all of your homework and are out on the water, having found the right conditions, what are you going to do about it? It's time to make some fishing decisions and get some bait in the water. This is the fun part. Time to drop the 'riggers and put 'em out! **SB**

**Sailfish certainly do cruise close to the beach. This sail was jumped off Boynton Beach, Florida in April.**

## CHAPTER 9

# Trolling Patterns and Spreads

It's been said that a day of big-game trolling boils down to eight hours of tedium broken by 15 minutes of pandemonium. Or something like that. Not so for sailfish, however.

A good trolling captain is constantly analyzing the water, looking for the best conditions. His crew is skilled at rigging baits, deploying lines and adjusting the spread. Teasers, which are various devices used to attract sailfish, come in many shapes and colors. They require specialized attention. Some crews like surface "chains," while others favor deep-running dredges. If news of a good bite crackles over the VHF, the team must be prepared to pull in the entire works and start again in new water.

There's plenty to keep you busy between bites, in other words.

And then the moment of truth: A purple missile in the boat wake; a sharp bill piercing the surface. Angler and crew jump to attention.

Game on.

## Reading the water: It isn't easy and takes some time to analyze.

See DVD for more on trolling patterns, spreads and teasers.

Slowing down at mid-day, the captain in a search mode. He's watching for sign: weedlines, free-jumping sailfish, color changes, temperature variations, even bottom structure.

# Old School Fishing

I n some parts of the world, the live versus dead bait argument can get pretty heated. There are some who think fishing with live bait is cheating and doesn't require skill. In turn, there are others who think trolling is "old school," a dated technique. It still pays for you to master both approaches and be confident when you make that choice. Let's first consider the benefits of trolling dead baits and why trolling has so many die-hard devotees.

Hookless ballyhoo teaser above lures sailfish in close for pitch-baiting with real hooks—like the circle-hook rigged ballyhoo, below.

Trolling rigged baits for sailfish clearly has its historical significance. The original sporting technique for catching sails dates back to the early part of the last century. While it may be difficult to imagine (with technology we have at our fingertips these days), it's easy to feel a connection with pioneers of this sport while trolling rigged, dead bait. If you made it as authentic as possible and only trolled plain, dead baits rigged on wire, without extra window dressing or teasers, you'd really be old school.

Then, of course, you couldn't use your electronics, either. Why handicap yourself like that? I don't know about you, but I want the most action I can pack into one day, while offshore. Regardless of how tricked-out our trolling techniques have become, deadbait trolling still feels like a link to the past. You will probably derive a greater sense of satisfaction out of catching sailfish on dead bait, due to the extra effort involved in just getting baits in the water. By first obtaining fresh dead bait such as ballyhoo, mullet or bonito strips, then prepping and rigging them correctly, you've already accomplished something pretty impressive.

Essentially, you're bringing a fish back to life when you rig a trolling bait. That's no easy feat for the beginner; rigging dead baits requires a fair amount of practice. Once you've mastered the steps of various rigs, you'll then want to work on your speed. This takes time and a level of commitment that most people don't

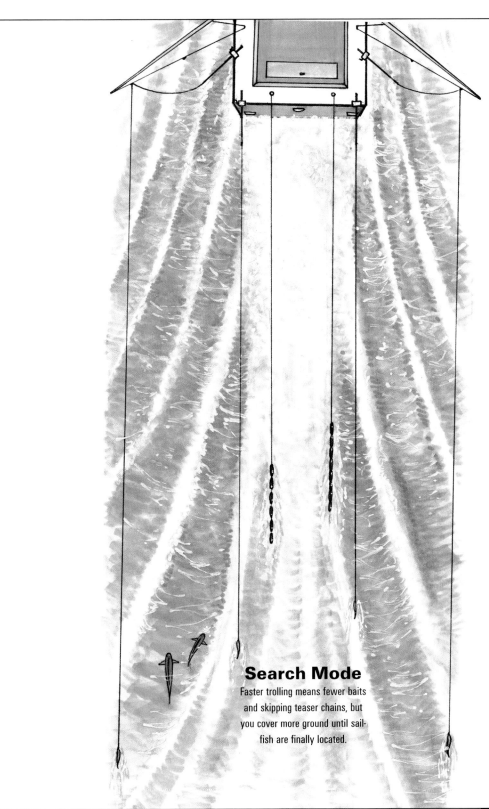

## Search Mode

Faster trolling means fewer baits and skipping teaser chains, but you cover more ground until sailfish are finally located.

**Today's more elaborate teaser systems, such as dredges and spreader bars, only complicate matters. They are a lot to handle at boatside.**

have these days. For sure, though, you're going to have a greater feeling of pride when you achieve success with baits you've rigged yourself. It may be this additional challenge we accept and its rewards that makes some folks

![PRO TIP] TEASERS

## Teaser Retrieval

Teasers can be one of the most important parts of your spread while sailfishing. Teasers can also be incredible nuisances, both to deploy and maintain. Today's more elaborate teaser systems, such as dredges and spreader bars, only complicate matters. They are a lot to handle at boatside and the many arms of a dredge frame increase the likelihood of problems with tangles and weeds fouling them. As a result, you are constantly pulling them in to check and repair them. You'll soon find out that this can drag down the program, if you're repeatedly slowing down the boat to reach out for teaser lines with a gaff, or turning away from the teaser to bring the line within reach for retrieval.

An easy fix to this problem is to add a retrieval ring to your outrigger line. Simply add a sliding line to the same guide in your outrigger you use for the teaser line, with a stainless steel or glass ring crimped onto it. With the teaser line fed through the ring, the line can be raised or lowered to bring your teaser line within easy reach of the cockpit. With heavier teasers such as natural dredges, this also makes it easier to pull the line in by hand—quicker than your teaser reels can do the job. For a simpler daisy chain teaser, it also allows you to bring a hot teaser fish inside the spread, closer to the corner of the transom. This enables an angler trying to switch a fish off the teaser and onto a hand-held flat bait, with better positioning for the fish to see your bait. SB

Plastic squid teasers retrieved.

die-hard, deadbait fans.

Another benefit of trolling dead bait is the ability to cover a lot of ground. There are times and places where you need to move across a significant amount of offshore real estate, before you see that first sailfish. Fishing an area that doesn't have a lot of what the pros call "coverage" can be a handicap. What they mean is a large number of boats can cover a wide area and eventually, someone finds the fish. Once that happens, they usually converge and try to catch more than one another. If you fish an area that doesn't have good coverage, it can take some time to locate the fish. Remember that you will be checking all known structures in the area and looking for water quality and bait. However, spread this out over miles of open ocean and it could take a while. The ability to cruise around hunting from one potential spot to another at three to six knots, with baits in the water, ensures you will be making better use of your time.

As to where to put your baits for the most attractive spread, most experts agree it varies from boat to boat. What you need to do is find your ideal "sweet spot" for short, medium and long baits, based on how your boat performs. Do the baits swim or skip through the water? Do they look natural? How far back each bait runs and from how high in the outrigger you pull it are important. Remember, you're trying to imitate a live fish. Baits that are jerking across the surface and stumbling end-over-end won't get much attention. Also, consider the visibility factor from a sailfish's perspective. Can the fish see all of your baits, or are they constantly swimming through the engine's whitewash? Finding locations at close, middle and long range, while keeping everything looking natural in clean water, is the first rule. This may vary from day to day based on sea conditions, as well. Declaring

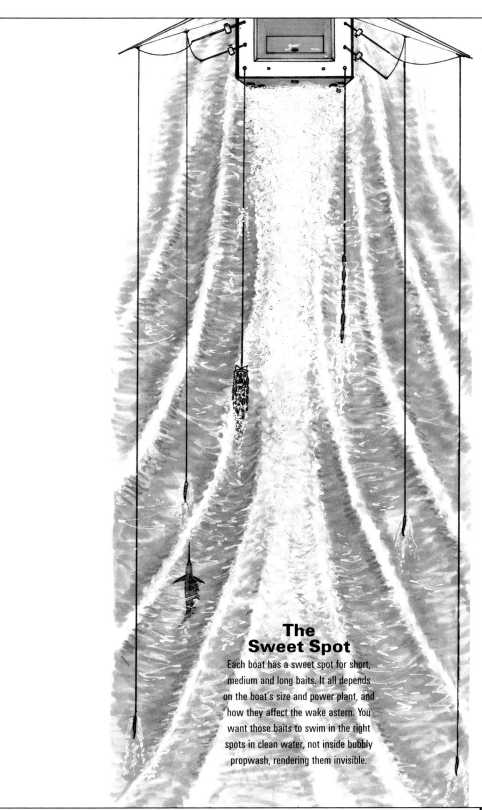

## The
## Sweet Spot

Each boat has a sweet spot for short, medium and long baits. It all depends on the boat's size and power plant, and how they affect the wake astern. You want those baits to swim in the right spots in clean water, not inside bubbly propwash, rendering them invisible.

exact bait distances is pointless without knowing the day's sea conditions. You have to find your boat's own sweet spots. This can vary from as little as 25 feet back for short lines, to 200 feet for the long "shotgun" bait.

There are some accepted guidelines for the arrangement of baits in the spread. Drag the baits at equal distances or staggered? That depends on how much turning you do. Staggering your baits spreads them out over a larger area. This increases the odds that if a fish pops up to check out the spread, there will be a bait near his face. It does, however, make it more difficult to make any radical turns. With your baits staggered at uneven intervals, turning sharply makes your lines turn independently, making them more prone to over-

## Move your spread around until it looks "right." You will know it when you see it.

lap and tangle. Baits pulled at similar distances (with short, middle and long lines even) will all turn nicely together—making them less prone to cross.

For this reason, find your best trolling bait patterns for rough weather and calm, and for running straight in a search mode, or circling a spot. Move your spread around until it looks "right." You will know that when you see it. When your spread resembles a live bunch of baitfish running for their lives or spooked by the boat running over them, you'll know it. Take the time to experiment with placement until you achieve that natural-looking presentation. Unlike an artificial lure whose realism is subjective, natural bait's realism is not open for interpretation. It either looks alive or it doesn't. Keep working at it until you're satisfied.

Whether it's out of a sense of tradition, convenience, or economics, and assuming we are going trolling today, where do we begin? Let's start out with a look at some typical trolling spreads and break down their effectiveness. Regardless of what you put in the water for baits, it's all a part of a larger system when you're trolling. Here's a breakdown of three

categories often used, depending on the conditions offshore:

## Trolling on the Go

The three modes you may get yourself into have a lot to do with how hard you're looking for sailfish. If you need to cover a lot of ground in a hurry, but don't necessarily want to steam around at cruising speed, you'll be trolling at the upper end of the speed limit for sailfish. Covering water at six to seven knots is really on the fast side for a sailfish. They will eat

Bigger boats jostle for position after several sailfish have just been sighted. Keep in mind that there are baits often far behind other boats; crossing wakes too close will result in cut lines. Courtesy is called for.

baits moving at this speed, but prefer things a little easier.

Trolling at this speed has disadvantages: For one thing, you will be pushing a lot of white-water, making it more difficult for sailfish to pick your baits out of the spread. You will also be "washing out" natural baits more quickly at this higher speed. It's less practical to pull any elaborate teaser arrangements at this speed and keep them in the water.

To keep things neat and organized at speed, move your spread back a bit farther behind the boat. It's easier to keep baits in the water, looking natural and somewhat out of the wash, if you stretch them back a little. A dredge teaser, which is normally run with some type of trolling lead ahead of it to keep it submerged, is probably not going to work when you need to cover ground. Running a simple four-to-six bait spread with a pair of daisy chains is fine for this method.

This type of speed is only necessary when you want to move around at a good clip. Going from spot to spot looking for surface

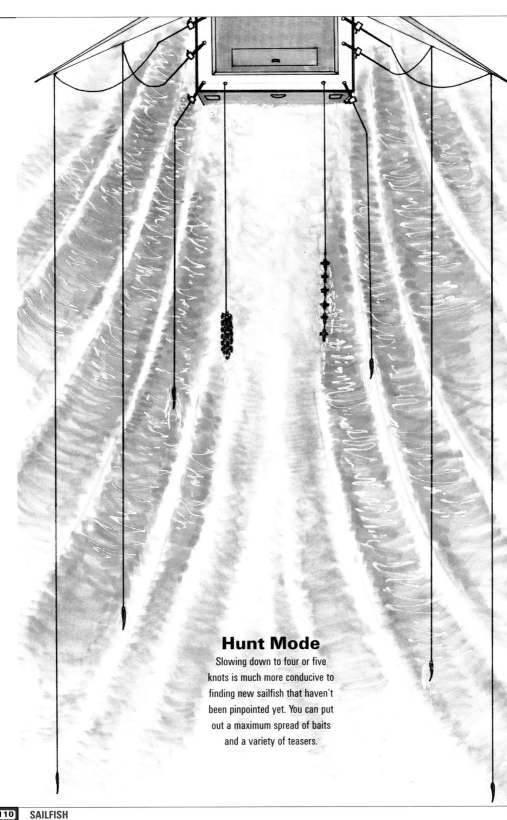

## Hunt Mode

Slowing down to four or five
knots is much more conducive to
finding new sailfish that haven't
been pinpointed yet. You can put
out a maximum spread of baits
and a variety of teasers.

activity, checking the bottom for baitfish and trying to locate ideal conditions worth slowing down for—that's all we're trying to accomplish. Some days you might never find some great scenario offshore, but still get those bites anyway. Sailfish on the move are most likely to jump your baits under these circumstances.

With migrating fish, it's more often a bite out in the middle of nowhere, with no obvious signs before the strike. If you're searching and get a bite out of seemingly empty water, that's a good time to slow down and analyze surrounding conditions. Move around at this speed until you have determined a *reason* to slow down and cover an area more effectively.

## Hunting Mode Means Slow it Down

Once you find a situation that warrants a closer look, you'll want to back off on those engine rpm's and really fish an area more carefully. This is when you get your real bait and teaser spread out behind the boat. Trolling at a more casual four to five knots is much more suitable for enticing sailfish. If you find water that looks right (for example a nice edge with a temperature break and scattered bait on the surface) you'll want to stay in this area and pick around more thoroughly. Now's the time to pull out all the stops.

A standard spread for sailfish trolling includes four to six baits. If your outriggers are long enough and allow it, use two long 'rigger baits and two short 'riggers, along with two flatlines. That's standard. You'll also want to run two teasers, one from each 'rigger, or one from a stern cleat or teaser rod in each corner. On some days, such as rough, windy weather or if you are short-handed for crew, this may be more than you want to deal with. Cutting back to four baits is fine if conditions are tough. If you must simplify your spread, consider it more important to keep your dredge teasers in the water, rather than two extra baits. Remember how much more of a visual attractor the dredge really is, with its 25- to 50-bait profile, than a single, hooked ballyhoo would be. It's always

easy to have a couple of extra rigged baits on a rod, stored in a cooler and ready to "pitch" to a fish that you raise on a teaser.

When you switch yourself into hunting mode, you should be trying to cover a general area very thoroughly until you raise a fish. This would include working over rips or edges on the surface with floating debris, or bait

# Mark Those Lines

Returning your bait to its ideal working position in the spread is important for a few reasons. First, you have already established a spot in the wake where the bait is most visible and swimming properly. Next, you have your spread dialed in so that nothing is becoming tangled during the boat's turns. And finally, you want to quickly get your lines back in working order, during a bait check or swap-out. This trick gets you back to the wheel quicker and more importantly, back to paying attention to the complete picture instead of a single detail.

When counting out the line "by hands," you are

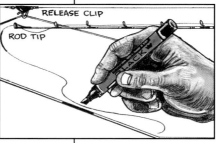

pulling line off the rodtip and dumping it into the water to get close to the same measurement each time. To fine-tune this even further, if you have a pattern that works all the time under any condition, mark the line at the exact spot where you clip it into a rigger or where it sits in the rodtip for flatlines. All it takes is a couple of passes over the line with a permanent black felt marker. These marks get you quickly back in action and are only semi-permanent. The mark will last a couple of days out in the sun and water and can be retouched if necessary or replaced with fresh marks, should you choose to change things up or cut back your lines to start over. **SB**

Three signs to watch for: Circling, fish-hunting frigatebird (above), weedlines and currents colliding, called "rips," (middle) and water color changes where coastal water meets cleaner water, often marked by sargassum.

## Too many anglers shut off their brains, once they locate fish sign.

scattered along their length. Fish an edge like this methodically. Try to determine where sailfish are likely working along its length, by covering one side of a blue-to-green water edge, then the other. Or move close to the edge and then farther away from it. That's leaving no stone unturned. Pay attention to details as you work the area, such as water temperature changes and how bait and birds are relating to the edge. By thinking about the details of your situation, you will have a better understanding when you do finally raise a sailfish. This makes it possible for you to get back in the same position and repeat the process, after you catch a fish. Too many anglers seem to shut off their brains, once they locate decent "fish sign." Try to understand why the bite took place, instead of just catching fish.

The same principle applies with underwater signs. Locating schools of baitfish beneath the surface is a good reason to slow down. Once

COLOR CHANGE

WEEDLINE FORMS ALONG CURRENT EDGE...

any significant amount of bait is marked on your bottom recorder, try to establish whether they're spread out over a wide area, or holding tight over solid structure. This is easily accomplished by watching your bottom machine and chartplotter simultaneously. Try to work in a search pattern and establish the limits of the area the baitfish are hanging around in. Also try to determine the attitude of the bait schools. Baitfish schools showing on your recorder as a loose, fragmented cloud—not tightly packed together—are probably not facing threats. A school of bait tightly packed, appearing on your screen as a solid red cloud, is more likely in a struggle for survival. This is an area that deserves a lot of attention.

Finally, a tightly packed school of baitfish showing up on the surface is a home run. Under these circumstances, you'll usually see sailfish feeding on them at the surface. Or at least, there will be an indication sails are feeding on them. First look right into the water for the fish, or on the surface. You may actually see sailfish physically finned out on top, slashing through bait pods. If you don't see the fish on top but baitfish are showering, something is usually pushing them up from below. A dead giveaway is when seabirds are allowed to pick away at baitfish on the surface, bait that refuses to dive deeper. Obviously, pressure to remain on the surface is coming from some bigger predator below.

Never run away from a scenario like this, without exhausting every option. If you find yourself fortunate enough to experience these conditions, it's time to go into the third mode.

## Camping Out

At this location you should be trying to stay right on top of the area without disrupting the feeding activity. To accomplish this, you'll need to work carefully around the out-

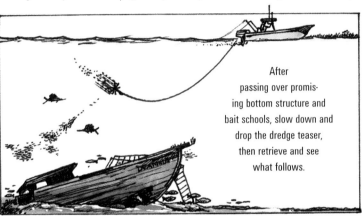

After passing over promising bottom structure and bait schools, slow down and drop the dredge teaser, then retrieve and see what follows.

skirts of the bait at first and try to tempt a fish out of the fray. This may even require you to further slow it down. Speeds as slow as one to three knots are not too slow under these conditions. If the baitfish pods cover only a small, very tight spot, it may even be necessary to bump the boat engines in and out of gear, allowing your spread to sink while you maintain position. Often you'll locate a school of bait on the surface getting thrashed from below. They may momentarily go deep once you start working around them, but this is where your dredge teasers come into play.

The actual name of the dredge teaser originates from its use. By rigging a dredge with a heavy cigar-shaped lead ahead of the actual frame, you can get it to sink down to a given depth. When baitfish are located holding deep over structure, being driven to the surface periodically by sailfish, try "dredging them up" within range of your bait spread. Work your way slowly into the current and/or wind and stop over the bait schools, allowing the dredges and your baits to sink down into the top of the baitfish school. By easing the boat ahead, you can sometimes bring the sailfish school right up to the surface. This often incites a flurry of action. Even if sails don't follow your dredges to the surface, the appearance that baitfish have broken away from their school (via the dredge) and are naturally more vulnerable, may be all it takes to turn these predators on. **SB**

# Rigging Natural Baits

**O**pinions vary widely on what exactly is the best spread to deploy, when trolling dead bait for sailfish. Many anglers will argue to the end about their favorite method, but the fact is there really isn't one magic pattern for all boats. Sharp captains will vary their spread constantly to suit changing conditions. Before you get locked into one particular setup, consider all the factors facing you.

This will largely depend on the sea state, your trolling speed and the type of baits you are offering. Two constants to bear in mind are that the baits should look as natural as possible at all times, and should always be highly visible to the fish you're targeting. By changing your spread to meet these needs as you change your attack plan, you're always going to be in the hunt.

## Rigging dead baits is an important part of the learning process.

DVD SPECIAL FEATURE: Detailed bait rigging.

Live bait has become so prevalent in some areas, many anglers believe sailfish won't eat a dead bait. The fish above proves otherwise.

# You Can't Beat Natural Baits

Y ou might be wondering while doing all of this hunting and exploring offshore, exactly what kind of baits you should be dragging. Although we've determined that a four- to six-line spread with teasers is the standard, you must also decide what kind of bait to use. And where exactly it will bounce along behind the boat. If you asked 50 of the most respected sailfish skippers in the world what they preferred to pull and in which position, each would answer a little differently. There are similarities and items many captains agree on, but each has his favorite setup. There is also the problem of matching baits for the correct situation offshore.

When sailfish are showering ballyhoo schools along the reef, you won't do as well when trolling something other than rigged ballyhoo past them. In fact, you might not even draw a strike. It may be that ballyhoo are plainly on the menu that day and exactly what the predators want.

**Ask 50 of the most respected sailfish skippers what they prefer to pull, an**

Get your spread fine-tuned first. The right baits in the proper location result in more bent rods. Select baits first, rig them properly and deploy them in the most visible location, for best success.

Those same 'hoos are generally good day in and day out, perhaps because of their oily taste. If color is key that day, a variety of colored skirts should get their attention. It may be that a purple skirt draws all the strikes that day.

On another day along the beach, if sails are whacking away at migrating mullet schools (common in November), then it pays off to have a few rigged mullet on the boat. Stay flexible; a few dead baits are easily rigged. If sailfish are balling up a tight school of sardines on the surface or around a sunken wreck, you know the drill—pull out the sabiki bait rigs and "match the hatch."

**ch will answer a little differently.**

## Bait Selection

The three most commonly used dead baits for sailfish are ballyhoo (above), mullet and strip baits. These baits are trolled around the world and for good reason: They're often readily available and they work. Of these three baits, one stands out as the most popular: The ballyhoo has probably accounted for more sailfish captures worldwide than any other bait. Maybe that's because 'hoos roam ocean reefs. More likely it's because they're easy to rig and look great in the water.

# Ballyhoo

**B**allyhoo are available packed according to size, a dozen per bag in countless bait and tackle stores. They range in size from small, 6-inch baits called "dinks" to full-grown baits of 12 inches and up known as "horse" baits. Ideal bait size varies, depending on where you fish. For Atlantic sails, anglers typically prefer small to medium-size baits. In

A large Pacific sailfish like this would have no trouble eating a horse ballyhoo.

## Ballyhoo Prep

By prepping baits you are trying to accomplish a few things. First, you're purging the stomach cavity of any waste and also popping out the inflated swim bladder.

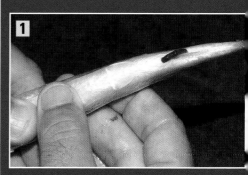

**1**

Holding the bait gently in your hand facing you and belly up, gently squeeze from the front of the bait's stomach and work from head to tail toward the vent. The stomach's contents will exit the bait through the vent.

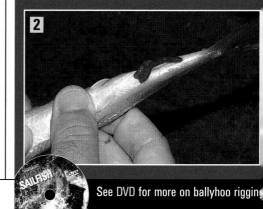

**2**

the Pacific where sailfish run considerably bigger, large or even horse ballyhoo work just fine. While even a small Atlantic sailfish can easily gobble a horse ballyhoo, the smaller baits are much preferred. The main reason is what we call the "edibility versus hookup ratio." Smaller baits are easier for a sailfish to catch and position in their mouths, before they swallow it head-first. Something can always arouse suspicion in the sailfish, causing it to spit the bait out before a hookup. Mouthing a large ballyhoo takes longer, delaying a hookup, when every second counts. Small baits are also easier to rig with a smaller hook, more appropriate in scale to the size of a typical Atlantic sailfish's mouth.

Ballyhoo do require a little preparation before rigging, to make them flexible and to give them a more natural "swimming" appearance. One thing to remember is that the amount of manipulation necessary to get that bait onto a leader can be a little rough, if it has

See DVD for more on ballyhoo rigging

Bright, fresh baits are always an advantage and will stand up to the preparation routine. They also troll far better than frozen bait.

**3**

Next, turn the bait belly down in your hand and gently pinch the top of its back, working from head to tail. This action should loosen up the backbone. You will notice the depression down the top center on the fish's back "pop up" as you go.

**4**

Finally, rinse the bait off in salt water and flex it loosely in a snakelike motion to complete. Before you attach this bait to a leader you should also remove the eyeballs to keep them from bulging out. This also provides an easy hole to pass your rigging wire through during the final rigging stage.

# Bull's Eye

Removing the eyes of a dead ballyhoo for trolling serves two purposes. Ballyhoo eyes, when left intact, have a tendency to bulge, causing the bait to spin. It's also easier to rig the copper wire through the open eye socket, rather than threading the wire around the eyeball. A handy device for removing the eyes and storing loose baits on is an old hunting arrow. Push an arrow through the eyes of your ballyhoo to route out the socket and stack them down the arrow's length to store in your bait cooler. Remember to leave the nock or insert on the end of the arrow to prevent the inside of the shaft from filling with the discarded byproduct and its resulting aroma.

By storing baits in this manner, you're able to lay the baits in the cooler on their backs. Shake a layer of kosher salt on their stomachs to toughen them up for trolling. It also makes it easier to keep them together in a bunch in the bottom of the cooler, while preventing loose baits from rolling around in the bottom of the box in melted icewater. When you need a fresh bait to rig, simply pull one off the end of the arrow and rig it. SB

# Mono Ballyhoo Rig

Always begin with the highest quality fresh bait, new leaders and sharp hooks. Small details make the difference at the moment of truth.

**1** Insert your hook into the gill opening and exit the center of the belly with the hook point while pulling the eye of the hook into the body cavity.

**2** Be sure the hook is lined up on the center line of the bait for straight tracking and that the throat latch isn't damaged. Bring the copper wire out of the bait through the eye socket.

**3** Keeping the wire tight, make two wraps around the lower eye socket and gills to anchor the hook in bait.

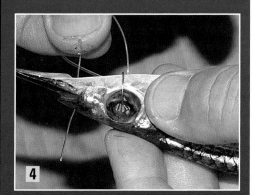

**4** Push the wire up through the lower jaw and exit through the top jaw where it joins the head. Pull tight.

been previously frozen.

Fresh bait is always superior, since the baits will look brighter and stand up better to the rigors of rigging and trolling them. Any time you have a chance to buy fresh ballyhoo rather than frozen, you should do so. Anglers who use a large number of these baits should consider buying a good supply of them while they're available and fresh. Do so for future outings, including the prep work before they're packaged for freezing.

Putting previously frozen baits through this process is a delicate matter. Frozen but thawed ballyhoo, if earlier frozen in superior condition, can stand up to this routine if you take a little extra care during the process. Sub-standard baits tend to fall apart if you try this. If you find yourself forced to settle for lesser quality baits, eliminate all but the snaking motion from the prep routine—and carry extra baits. Lesser quality baits fall apart more quickly in the water. You can plan for this by packing along more than you think you will need. Remember to thaw your baits slowly by submerging them in salt water. Always let them thaw completely, before you try any of these steps, including the rigging. Rushing the process will only degrade bait integrity and cause them to wash out quicker behind the boat.

**5** Make a couple of wraps down the beak and stop. Break the beak short and split the beak with your leader. Pull leader up into the split. Wrap the copper wire over the split and continue wrapping forward to the end. Leader exits at an angle from the top, causing the bait to dig in and swim.

# Circle Hook **Ballyhoo** Weighted

As circle hooks become more popular for both live baiting and trolling, many new tricks for rigging baits with them are being developed along the way. A popular technique for rigging ballyhoo for trolling involves preparing the baits without a leader attached. This method makes it much neater and keeps your bait cooler more organized.

This approach is standard in Central America, where several dozen baits per day are required. It keeps the baitbox free of tangled leaders when the action gets hot. This rig is quick and easy and works like a champ for rigging a leaded "swimming ballyhoo." See the DVD for an alternative method using copper rigging wire; both rigs are extremely effective.

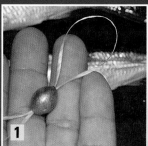

**1** Begin by doubling 2 feet of waxed rigging line and passing looped end through small egg sinker.

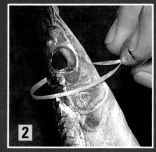

**2** Pull the looped end over the bait's head and slip it under the gill plates on both sides of the bait.

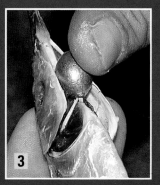

**3** Slide the egg sinker down the rigged line so it fits between the gills forward of throat latch.

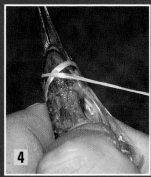

**4** Bring the line's ends forward under the bait's lower jaw and wrap over top jaw. Keep line tight.

DVD SPECIAL FEATURE: Exclusive circle hook and split bill ballyhoo rigging techniques.

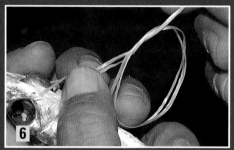

**5**

Pass both ends through eye sockets from opposite directions. Wrap gills over sinker and knot tight.

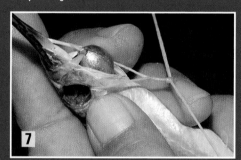

**6**

Tie another overhand knot in the two strands of line and pull it tight.

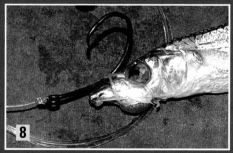

**7**

Pull the two ends away from each other; knot will slip down to egg sinker. Snug up and trim.

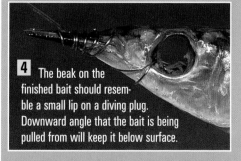

**8**

To complete, break the beak off short and insert circle hook under x-shaped loop of thread on top of head.

# Split Bill Ballyhoo

This extra step, added to a standard mono-rigged bait, will turn skipping surface baits into head-down swimmers. Being head-down gives it a swimming plug-like action without extra weight. They are so effective, they may be the most commonly used rig of all. Their simplicity to rig and life-like action are tough to beat.

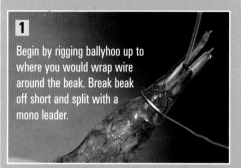

**1**

Begin by rigging ballyhoo up to where you would wrap wire around the beak. Break beak off short and split with a mono leader.

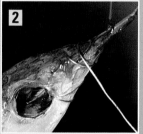

**2**

Continue wrapping the wire forward and lift the mono leader so you can wrap the wire in front of it.

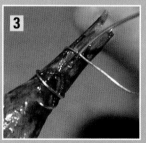

**3**

Make a single wrap in front of the leader and finish wrapping back toward the bait's mouth until you are out of wire.

**4** The beak on the finished bait should resemble a small lip on a diving plug. Downward angle that the bait is being pulled from will keep it below surface.

# Strip Baits

Strip baits, which are cut from bonito sides and bellies, may be the most underrated trolling bait available for sailfish. They have long been a favorite for charterboats due to their low cost and effectiveness, and originate from the ready supply of little tunny or

Few baits can match the hookup ratio of a strip bait.

"false albacore" found throughout the Atlantic sailfish's range. One of the most attractive features of the strip is the elimination of (or at least reduction in) the "whiff factor." When a sailfish eats almost any other trolled bait, following the dropback, if the rod isn't bent, you generally don't get another shot at that fish. Or not with that bait, anyway. In offshore circles this is referred to as a whiff. With a ballyhoo bait, you usually end up with just a head and a hook left behind, also known as a "san cocho" named after a Latin seafood dish made with fish heads. With a strip, on the other hand, if you whiff a shot at a sailfish, the bait will stay intact long enough for one or more chances at the very same fish. (How cool is that?)

In fact, a sailfish that has a strip pulled out of its mouth will often come back even hotter the second time, if the bait is cranked back to the surface as if it escaped. Another benefit of using a strip is that your hookup rate will climb sharply. Consider what a flat piece of belly skin with a razor sharp hook in it offers a sailfish: Mostly a hook, is what the fish get for their effort. The slim profile of a strip bait doesn't impede the hook's path into the fish's mouth.

## Prepping the Fillet for Strips

1

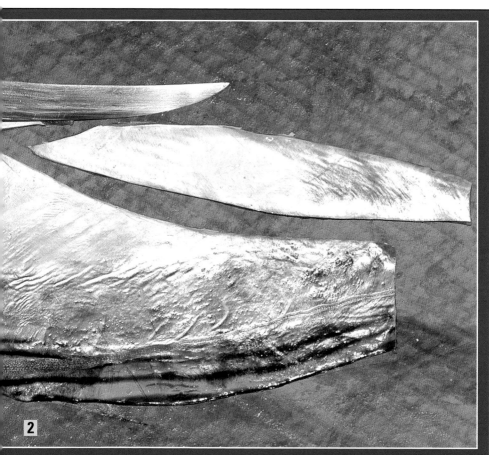

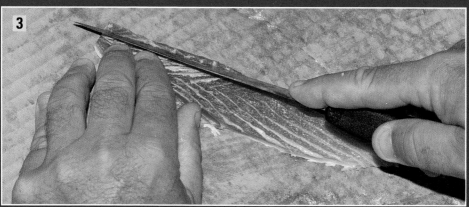

**1** Start by cutting the bonito side down to 1/4 inch thick. Next, scrape the fillet down to flatten and produce an even thickness. Always follow the grain of the meat.

**2** Next, cut individual baits out of each side in the shape of a willow leaf. Baits can range in size from 4 to 8 inches. Plan your cuts carefully to get the most baits possible from each slab.

**3** Fine-tune each bait to remove any ragged edges and bevel the edges of the meat, to improve action. Square off the forward point of the bait so it's pulled along with the grain.

Strip baits are also easy to store and can be stacked up in flat packages without taking up the entire freezer. They also take up very little room in a bait cooler and can be re-frozen without suffering much loss of quality, even after a couple of trips.

The standard sailfish strip is cut into a willow leaf shape with the leading tip squared off and the trailing tip left either pointed or split into a fork-tail. Sailfish strips are usually cut between six and nine inches long, but can be tailored to suit a situation if necessary. For example, in the early part of the sailfish run on the Southern U.S. Atlantic coast, you often see quite a few juvenile sailfish before the main run gets under-way. These little "snakes," only three to four feet long, can test the patience of even the saltiest angler. The problem with such small fish is they have a hard time dealing with large baits and will go from one to the next, mutilating and spitting them out along the way, never quite getting the hook. To remedy this problem you can cut some short little 4-inch strips and rig them with smaller 4/0 hooks and get a solid

# Rigging Strip Baits

**1** Start by making a minimal small hole in the front of the bait, to pass your leader through.

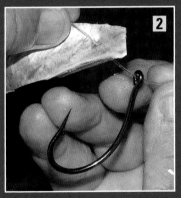

**2** Pass your leader through the bait and your hook. A loop knot such as the perfection loop shown is used to finish the rig. A crimp may also be used for heavier leaders.

**3**

DVD SPECIAL FEATURE: Exclusive strip bait rigging techniques.

hookup on these younger spindlebeaks.

A strip bait also requires a shorter dropback. The instant a sailfish has the bait in its mouth you should be getting tight. There is no actual baitfish to turn around into position for swallowing here, just some flavored skin and a hook. A flatline strip bait should be freespooled quickly and the reel locked up fast, while a 'rigger bait can even be fished with the reel always locked up, using just the delay when the line falls out of the clip for a dropback.

Unlike ballyhoo or mullet, which are attrac-

tive offerings fished plain or naked, a strip bait must be dressed up with some type of enhancer. Various Sea Witch or feather-type lures are preferred to cover the front of a strip and give it more bulk. Remember when choosing an attractor for strips, not to go overboard. It's important to maintain the slim profile around the hook area to preserve the most appealing feature of the bait itself, which is easy hookups. Surrounding the bait with too much rubber and tinsel defeats the original purpose of using this bait.

# Dress Up Your Strip Bait

Small squid skirts and Sea Witches finish off a strip nicely. Add a lure only for color. Large, bulky lures will impede the hookup ratio of the bait and diminish its effectiveness.

# Mullet

Mullet have a long history as a sailfish bait. In the earliest days of rod and reel action on these fish, you trolled mullet. The common bait of that bygone, Crunch and Des era was a simple deboned silver mullet rigged on wire. Originally, it was commercial king mackerel fishermen being pestered by sailfish that sparked an interest in trying to catch sailfish. They disliked the fact that sailfish would ruin their rigged mullet, leaving them with nothing to show for their effort. Logically,

Stack of mullet ready to de-bone before going offshore.

sports anglers began targeting sails with the same baits, while trying to fine-tune techniques for hooking more sailfish. What has become apparent over the decades since then is that mullet may be good for raising sailfish, but they're not so great for hooking them.

The solid profile and tough bone structure of an adult silver mullet is a hindrance to the hook finding its way into a sailfish's mouth. Mullet have a tendency to get balled up around the hook during the dropback process. Smart bait fishermen then figured out a way to fillet a mullet from the inside to remove the backbone and entrails, while splitting the tail into two separate, filleted strips. The split-tail mullet was born.

Despite the fact this technique greatly improves the hookup ratio, a gradual turn away

## Salting Baits

Deboned mullet ready for salting in body cavity. This works much better with fresh mullet, of course.

Use coarse kosher salt liberally to cure mullet baits and strips alike. Salt will remove moisture from baits.

Flesh of jelly-like consistency will turn tough and durable, like partially cured beef jerky.

# Prepping the Split Tail Mullet

**1**

Cut a diamond-shaped hole in top of bait. With a paring knife, cut inside from above the eyes back to the gills.

**2**

With a flexible fillet knife, make a cut between dorsal and anal fin as though you were filleting the bait.

**3**

Run the knife toward the tail, filleting only to the base of the tail.

**4**

Angle the blade downward and cut into the bone at the base of the tail.

**5**

Carefully slice back through the tail, separating into two separate laminates. This cut takes a little practice.

**6**

Next, insert knife up into body cavity and slice out the backbone, ribs and excess meat and entrails.

**7**

Pull out this plug and a flat, hollow mullet remains. Rinse out and salt the inside liberally before freezing.

**8**

Plug removed. Always freeze before rigging hooks, to allow bait to cure.

DVD SPECIAL FEATURE: Exclusive split tail mullet prepping techniques.

from using large baits for sailfish has evolved. While still popular as a sailfish attractor on dredge teasers because of their high visibility, bigger mullet are not quite as popular as baits. Smaller juvenile "super-sail" mullet are still popular, however. These baits, measuring between four and six inches, are prepared a little

Split-tail mullet can be readily converted into hookless dredge baits by rigging on a short piece of wire.

differently. Rather than splitting the tail and knifing out the body cavity from the inside, split them lengthwise down the center of the back. The bulk of the meat and bones are removed through the top of the bait and the tail is left intact. This "cutback mullet" can be used more effectively, since there is less bait to prevent the hook from finding its mark. They may be rigged with the hook facing up or down and when combined with a small egg sinker under the chin, will swim more aggressively than any live mullet.

When cutting a supply of small mullet, it's important to salt the inside of the body cavity and freeze them once before use. Salting a bait such as a mullet or strip bait will cure the meat and toughen it, changing the texture of the bait from a mushy consistency to a tougher, more leathery meat. This greatly improves the bait's duration and effectiveness. Simply shake a little coarse kosher salt over the exposed meat of the bait before freezing.

# Rigging the Split Tail Mullet

Begin by making a split in the bottom of the bait between the ventral fins to pass the hook through.

Pass the eye of the hook up through the opening and continue out through the wedge head opening.

Insert the leader end through hook eye, into the head and exit through the gills. Pass leader end through a...

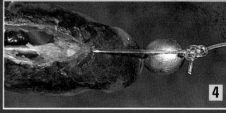

...small 1/8 -1/4 ounce egg sinker and place lead under chin of mullet. Tie loop knot or crimp to finish.

Egg sinker keeps rigged mullet bait from skipping too high, down where the sailfish can reach it.

## Closing the Gap

To complete the rig, you'll need to tie the wedge closed. This step gives the bait a flat profile which makes it track straight and keeps it from washing out.

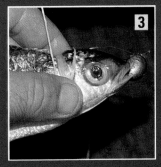

Tie the wedge cut closed by wrapping several turns around head with waxed rigging line and finish with tight overhand knots. Flatten head of bait on its side with palm of hand, before tightening rigging line.

Finished product is streamlined and ready to swim behind the boat.

# Prepping
# Cut Back Mullet

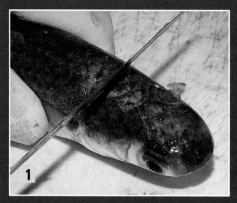

Head scales are removed, to facilitate a clean penetration from the hook. You wouldn't want a scale to foul the hook point, when a sailfish strikes.

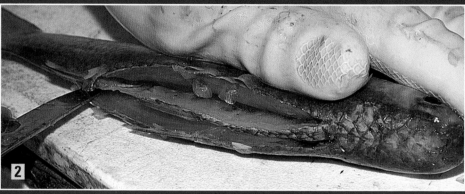

To prepare and "knife out" a cut-back mullet, simply fillet down both sides of the backbone and remove backbone, ribs and excess meat through the top of the bait. Like split-tails, these cut-backs should be salted and frozen before use.

Cleaned out body cavity, minus backbone and undesirable products that can cause spoilage. This is where the salt goes, to toughen the bait.

# Rigging Cut Back Mullet

This is another option for rigging dead mullet, a very sturdy bait that will swim for hours behind the boat. With practice, it only requires a few minutes to rig, before leaving the dock.

Since the head isn't wedged out, poke a hole in the head to guide leader through, at forward edge of eyes.

Insert eye of hook into incision and push forward, exiting out of the gill.

Lay hook along bait with eye of hook even with hole in top of head to locate where hook shank will exit.

Insert leader down through hole in head and out through gill opening, eye of hook and small egg sinker.

Make small incision in bottom of bait.

Finish with a perfection loop knot or crimp. No tying is necessary, since head is not wedged open.

# CHAPTER 11

# Livebait Rigs and Techniques

**F**ishing for sailfish has evolved over the years in many ways, but nothing has impacted the sport more than the use of live bait. It's created a source of controversy over which method—live bait or trolling dead—is more sporting.

Debate goes on over which method causes greater harm to the fish, too. It's been argued that live baiters have a tendency to accidentally injure or kill more sailfish, than do dead bait fisherman. This is pure fallacy—the key factor at work here is the length of dropback time allowed. It's as easy to overfeed and gut-hook a fish on dead, trolled bait as it is with live bait. It's certainly possible that a fish hooked beneath a kite flown too far from the boat, or a long shotgun 'rigger bait trolled way back, are allowed unnecessary time to consume the bait. Both are factors that can be controlled. It's up to us as responsible anglers and stewards of the fishery, to make every effort not to over-feed a fish and gut-hook it.

## It's hard to beat live baits. An entire fishery has evolved around them.

Nope, not going this way!
Sailfish inspects a nervous
baitfish that reverses course. A
livewell full of baits helps ensure
a productive day offshore.

# Keeping Baits on the Fish

The plain truth is that using live bait under many circumstances is the best way to get the most bites. A perfect example of this is when fishing an area crowded with boats using live baits. You will find it very difficult to compete with this fleet, if you try to troll among them. Livebait fleets tend to fish very close together and sit right on top of the action. A boat trolling through a tight crowd will only get in the way. Another example: You may find sailfish holding tight over a small area—sails concentrating on a dense bait school that won't

## The act of lifting hooked baitfish often triggers a feeding frenzy.

leave a wreck, for instance, or fish cutting up a surrounded bait school on the surface. There's a big difference between trolling in circles or setting up passes at the fish, compared to backing up to these fish and casting live baits to them. The amount of time these fish spend actually looking at a bait is much greater, if you're parked on top of them. They have more time to eat.

Live bait isn't the best approach on those days when you want to cover a lot of ground, obviously. But on days when you do find the fish and know right where you want to be, live bait is impossible to beat. An ideal scenario is finding sailfish feeding on surface schools of bait. If you can catch a supply of the same bait they're feeding on, (perhaps at the same location) and offer it back to them, well, it doesn't get any better than that. Some of my most memorable days offshore were spent doing exactly that. The bait is right there, and the act of lifting strings of struggling baitfish from a tightly packed school of fish often triggers a feeding frenzy. It's not uncommon to have sailfish follow a baitfish-loaded sabiki rig right to the back of your boat. Keeping sailfish rods rigged and ready while you're loading up your livewell is certainly wise.

There are a number of ways to present a

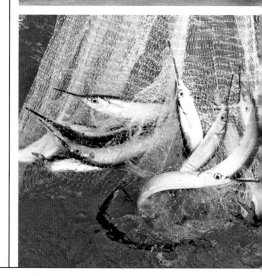

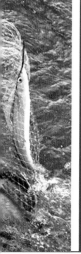

South Florida classic cold front conditions (above), combined with a good supply of live bait (left) leads to fast action and multiple sailfish hookups. Don't forget foul-weather gear during winter, even in Florida.

spread of live baits to sailfish. Like a dead trolling bait, they all have a specific application. The three most common techniques for deploying live baits are from outriggers as when trolling, drifting with the boat engines shut down, or under fishing kites. It's also possible to combine two methods simultaneously if you have plenty of help on the boat. The main consideration as to why you would choose one technique over the other is the amount of ground you intend to cover and how many lines you can handle in the water. Whether one method is more effective than another is subject to debate. Personally, I've seen days where they've each been the clear winner. Once again it's wise to learn how to do all three—and decide which method suits you best. Each can be very effective.

## Outrigger Fishing

This is a smart choice on days where conditions dictate you target an area very thoroughly. On days where you want to ease around in circles over an area, you obviously can't keep your bow pointed into the wind all the time and still make a circle. A kite requires facing into the wind, so you can see the dilemma. There are also days where you find a particular condition such as a current edge or rip, running across rather than parallel to the wind. If you want to work along its length and keep the kite in the air, you'll have problems. Other days there is no wind. Some people insist on attaching a helium balloon to their kite aloft on windless days, but I think you should know when to say when. This can turn into a situation where the tail wags the dog. I like to make decisions about where we're fishing rather than letting the kite decide for me. All of these scenarios are situations when it's wise to fish the baits from your outriggers.

## Bump-Trolling with Outriggers

Fishing live bait from outriggers is really not much different from trolling dead bait. It's simply done slower and more deliberately. It's pos-

sible to fish the exact same line and teaser arrangement as you deploy with dead bait, only substituting live fish for dead ones. A term commonly used to describe outrigger fishing with live bait is "bump trolling," which is nothing more than bumping the boat's engines in and out of gear as you go. The reason why

**There are three common techniques for deploying live baits: From outriggers when trolling, drifting with the boat's engines shut down, or drifting and/or slow-trolling with kites.**

you wouldn't stay in gear constantly is that the baits can't be pulled continuously without twirling or running out of energy and dying. A more natural presentation is to allow them the freedom to swim around on their own, only putting the boat in gear when you need to keep the lines from crossing. One of the bene-

fits of this method is that it offers the ability to troll baits in virtually any direction. Where a lot of turning and doubling back is required, this is very effective.

To deploy a spread of baits for bump-trolling, set up those lines as you would for deadbait trolling, four to six baits and two

Slick calm weather is the ideal condition to put the outriggers down and really cover some water.

**A nervous bait is an indication that it's seen something it doesn't care for at all. A bite very likely is only moments away.**

teasers. With your spread in the water, begin by stretching the lines out by moving the boat ahead slowly until they're nearly tight. Stop the boat and watch your lines. As the boat starts to drift off to the downwind side, your lines will begin to converge. Before the lines can tangle, bump the engines into gear and repeat the process. You are only moving ahead fast enough to keep those live baits from creating mischief. When you need to turn or circle, use the same technique. Everything is done gradually. For advanced warning when your baits are getting nervous, pay attention to your release clips on the outrigger lines. The clips should only be raised roughly three quarters of the way to the tip of the 'rigger poles. With the play in the 'rigger lines above and below the clips, you will see the clip shaking and stretching out the line as your bait gets nervous. This is an indication that the bait has seen something below it doesn't care for at all. A bite very likely is only moments away.

An alternate form of bump-trolling, called power-drifting, is useful when you're ready to cover some ground and still want the flexibility of turning and circling back. A power drift is identical to bump-trolling, except the boat is allowed to move along with the current and the wind, certainly more so than just kicking the engines in and out of gear. Those engines are only used to keep the boat facing into the current. The baits remain behind the boat. Power-drifting allows you to move along with the current and cover territory, while not placing extra strain on the baits by dragging them around. Once a spot of interest is discovered, you simply turn the boat around into the wind (and current) and go back to bump-trolling to explore the area more thoroughly.

**PRO TIP** DRIFTING DEEP BAITS

## Drift a Deep Bait

Often a deep line is just the ticket when sailfish aren't cooperating on the surface. For example, on a slick calm summer day when nothing seems to be happening, deep baits have saved many a day. There are a number of ways to deploy sub-surface baits with various swivel rigs and downriggers etc. The only problem with swivel rigs is that the lead remains attached and when a hooked fish jumps, will swing back and forth, perhaps working the hook out of the fish. With downriggers, if you're drifting with a live bait, the bait has a tendency to swim to the cable and ball and wrap up in a tangle.

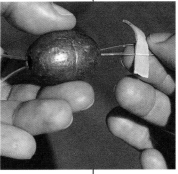

A great way to overcome these obstacles is to use a breakaway egg sinker while drifting. The simplest method for fixing a lead to your leader in this manner is by using a short length of rubber band. Cut a piece of rubber band (No. 32 or 64, depending on the size of the egg sinker hole) long enough to pass doubled, through the center of an egg sinker. Pull a doubled section (loop) of your leader, roughly 10 feet from the bait through one end of the sinker. Put the rubber band through the loop of leader line and pull both ends of mono loop back into the center of the egg sinker. By pulling the doubled leader and the rubber band into the lead, the snug fit will keep the lead in place on the leader. Any strain on both ends of the leader coming out of the lead will pull the rubber band through and release the sinker. You are then free to fight the fish with the outcome unaffected by additional weight.

## Dead-Boat Drifting With a Kite

A popular choice with anglers in open, center console boats is drifting with the engines off. On days when there are no obvious signs, drifting is a good option. Open boats with 360-

When the weather and ocean liven up, drifting with a sea anchor and fishing with a kite is much more comfortable for small boats.

degree walkaround configuration are ideal for this. Unlike a boat that limits fishing to the cockpit only, walkaround boats let you drift in the trough and fish off both sides of the boat. This requires rod holders lining both gunwales, port and starboard. Drifting with the waves allows you to fly a kite on your downwind side, while drifting flatlines and deep baits on the upwind side. This not only lets you fish more lines at once, it spreads your baits over a wider area. The benefit of having baits cover the water both 200 feet ahead and behind your drift is substantial. By covering up to 400 feet of water, you greatly increase the chance that a sailfish swimming by will run into one of those baits.

A typical spread for this type of fishing would include a kite flown downwind with two baits fished under it, with long and short flatlines on the upwind side as well as a deep line. Some very ambitious anglers, if they have the manpower on board, will fish two kites with two lines hung from each—as well as several flat and deep lines. This requires practice and a generous supply of bait, for starters. Never get more lines in the water than you can handle. It's counter-productive if you spend the entire day untangling lines and chasing after kites that crashed in the drink, each time you get a bite.

## A drift anchor allows you to fly a kite downwind, with flatlines and deep baits on the upwind side.

### Bump-Trolling With Kites

Kite fishing isn't limited to boats with walkaround ability. You can also troll live baits behind your boat with one or more kites as well. Combining kite baits with outrigger baits allows you to add more lines to the spread, than strictly outrigger fishing would. By adding a single kite line down the center of a standard bump-trolling setup, you can get two more baits in the water. Many boats fish two kites behind the boat and combine them with two short 'rigger lines and a flatline. Again, this is something you work up to.

The upside of kite fishing is in the presentation. Kite-flown baits are kept on the surface, swimming helplessly in circles. This surface action draws a lot of attention and the nervous vibration is certainly an attraction to predators. Additionally, most of your line and hardware are kept out of the water, away from the sailfish's line of sight. By contrast, once you have this many lines in the air and water, the kites are running the show. Your mobility is greatly reduced and the tendency to want everything to keep running smoothly can out-weigh the desire to investigate something fishy that isn't down-wind. Once again, it is a matter of considering the circumstances and choosing what will work best.

Regardless of which technique you choose after experimenting with each, you'll find a

A happy lad with his first sailfish in 1980, kept for the taxidermist. Was that the BeeGees playing in the background? Fiberglass mounts are the rule today.

decided preference. Not everyone enjoys switching methods at each turn of the wind or tide. Knowing that will keep you sharper and more committed to making things happen. You might find your boat is not ideally suited for all techniques, anyway. When you become familiar with what works best, you will ultimately succeed. Remember that at the end of your line is the same bait, regardless of the technique. If you offer sailfish what they want to eat, they'll cooperate—regardless of how you present it.

# The Bait

**P**robably the most important piece of the puzzle to solve while livebait fishing is the choice of baits. Sailfish are known to eat a wide variety of items, of course. As varied as their diet may be, there are days when one type of bait is all they want. You

## All the common types of baitfish used

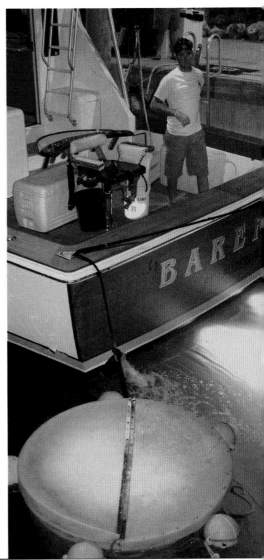

may have a livewell full of baitfish that sailfish couldn't eat fast enough a week ago, but today they won't give it a second glance. The best way to avoid this problem is to become familiar with the local bait supply and learn how to catch or procure them. Figure out how to grab a supply of bait at a moment's notice.

You may have already started your day by catching bait at one location and now have a full livewell. Despite this, any time you arrive in an area where sailfish have been seen or caught and baitfish is plentiful, be ready to catch more. If you determine your captured baits are the same as what's on the menu that day, so much the better. If not, be ready to catch what is.

All common types of baitfish used for catching sailfish are fairly easy to catch. They fall into three groups and are described in the next six pages.

## atching sailfish are fairly easy to catch. They fall into three groups.

Having lots of frisky live baits is a distinct advantage. Catching your own allows you to load the baitwell without draining your pockets. Some captains won't contaminate a live bait with bare hands, using a hook-out tool instead. A live pen back at the dock is useful to hold extra baits for the next day or when bait fishing gets tough, while trying to stockpile enough bait for a long weekend.

# Hard Baits

The first and most infamous bait would have to be the goggle-eye. This small member of the jack family has gained a reputation as the nectar that all sailfish love to eat. It also happens to be the baitfish that people line up to spend hundreds of dollars on, in the inlets each morning. Goggle-eyes are an ideal choice of bait for several reasons: They're the right size, for starters. When considering a

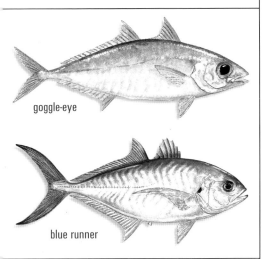

goggle-eye

blue runner

The value of healthy live bait is evident here. Anglers in South Florida have paid as much as $300 for a dozen goggle-eyes during a big tournament.

bait choice for sailfish, you should choose bait small enough for sailfish to eat quickly—yet large enough to troll around for a while and not expire from the strain. You also want a baitfish lively enough to attract attention, but not so athletic that a sailfish will give up trying to catch it. It should also be something a sailfish finds edible, of course. A bright, silver color certainly helps, too. Goggle-eyes meet all of these requirements.

I'm not sure if these facts make google-eyes worth the high retail price they command, however. The reason most people don't catch their own goggle-eyes is the fact you have to fish for them at night. Sleep can be precious; most folks are simply unwilling to leave the dock hours before daylight to catch their bait, then spend the rest of the day fishing. This is especially unappealing, when you know a bait boat is waiting at the inlet after daylight breaks, with a livewell full of frisky baits. For this reason, most people simply buy these primo baits. If you're ready to lose extra sleep and try it on your own, "gogs" are not especially difficult to catch. They're commonly found feeding around inshore rockpiles after dark. If you live close to where they're commonly caught and sold, a trip beyond the inlet before daylight with a supply of size 10 or 12 sabiki rigs will be worth the trouble. Find the inshore reefs and scattered structure and watch your depth recorder closely. Goggle-

Goggle-eye at top is mixed in with Spanish sardines. Notice how sturdy the "gog" is. They also have remarkable energy, much like a blue runner.

## Stay Ahead

When drifting or slow-trolling live baits for sailfish, a common scenario is for a fish to suddenly come up jumping before you even realize you're getting a bite. Sometimes you may be aware of an impending bite and the same thing happens. Fish that come in hot and eat your baitfish while it's trying to sprint back to the boat are tough customers. What most commonly happens is that your bait, while heading for the boat, creates a belly in the leader as it gets ahead of the leader and line. This belly is what the sailfish has to swim into while trying to catch its lunch. The result is usually the sailfish getting tangled in the leader and trying to jump out of the whole mess, ultimately freeing itself.

To avoid this situation, you should always be adding a little strain to your lines to stretch them out when a fish is chasing your bait. You

eyes will be scattered marks found throughout the water column. It pays to have a bright spreader light on the boat to attract them to the surface. The baits will often rise to the light as you lift a string of them from the bottom. They'll stay with your boat until you've caught enough for the day.

As daybreak arrives, if the goggle-eyes weren't cooperative, you'll get a shot at their less desirable cousins, blue runners. Similar to goggle-eyes and another member of the jack family, runners are often mixed in with them. They also feed all day around buoys and offshore towers. Sailfish will happily eat a small blue runner and they fit part of the description of the ideal bait. The runner's one shortcoming is the fact they're more athletic than a goggle-eye. Runners have this bad habit of running to the boat and hiding when they sense danger. They often do this little trick so quickly, you scarcely notice until it's too late. Many a runner has died bravely in a boat propeller, while a sailfish watched helplessly from a distance of only 10 feet behind the boat. For this reason, you must pay very close attention to your lines while using them for bait. Another smart option is to reserve blue runners for the long 'rigger baits or kite baits. A size 6/0 or 7/0 livebait hook is appropriate for baits in this size range. You can always clip off half the runner's boney tail to slow him down, so he won't sprint back to the boat.

Stay in contact with the fish during a dropback. Fish feeding toward the boat can be tricky.

don't have to drag the bait through the water. Try instead to keep a strain on the belly before it forms. Whether you stretch the line out with the forward motion of the boat or by simply reeling in the slack as it comes is unimportant, just do it. This can spell the difference between a fish you released and one you jumped off.

# Soft Baits

For those who like to get a little extra shut-eye before a day on the rip, there are a variety of scaled baits available after the sun clears the horizon. Spanish sardines, thread herring and pilchards are all popular choices for catching sailfish. These baits concentrate around nearshore structure, as well as on tidelines around inlets. The advantage of using these small, soft baits is their edibility. Sailfish can easily catch and consume

Popular baitfish spots can get tight. It pays to have a few secret spots to catch bait away from the crowd.

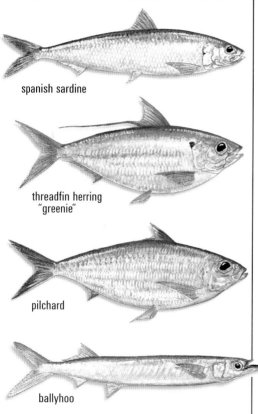

spanish sardine

threadfin herring "greenie"

pilchard

ballyhoo

them in one bite. Your hookup ratio should be a little better using these "one-biters," since the likelihood of a sailfish spitting them out, or your hook getting turned around into the bait during the dropback, is less.

To locate and catch these daytime baits, search around the inshore area where structure

or tidelines exist and watch your depth recorder, while also looking for bird activity. If you see a cluster of big boats within sight of the inlet, in waters of 30 feet or less, chances are they've found the baitfish schools. Seabirds also give up baitfish locations, since these baits spend a lot of time on or near the surface while feeding. Smaller-size sabikis such as Nos. 4 to 8 are more effective here. On days where you are seeing the baits but they won't eat, it pays to downsize the bait rig to a No. 4 to get more bites. If they are eating readily, the No. 8 hooks are more durable and won't straighten out under the strain of a load of baits.

These baits aren't as hardy as the larger hard baits mentioned earlier and will expire more quickly. You also need to fish them more slowly and delicately, to keep them frisky and natural-looking. If you elect to use soft baits, plan on carrying extra baits to ensure a supply that will last through the entire day. A size 4/0 to 6/0 livebait hook is perfect for these smaller baits.

**hools spooky and more difficult to stay on top of.**

## Toss a Livie

Pitch baits are one of the most exciting parts of the billfish experience. Any time you use one you are throwing the bait at a fine gamefish you've seen on the surface and adrenaline is usually running high. It's critical to always have those rods ready to go at a moment's notice. The opportunity

to hand-toss a livie to a passing sailfish simply won't wait for you to get a rod rigged up. If you're ready for such a fish and take advantage of the moment, your day can suddenly become a lot more exciting.

One of the more common scenarios you'll see is where the baitfish hits the water running near a sailfish—and shoots right back to the boat to hide. More often than not the sailfish won't follow and you've lost your chance. To avoid this, try hooking your pitch bait in the tail. Tail-hooked baits are not only more cast-friendly, since they travel through the air head-forward, they're also easier to steer. With the line pulling on the tail, the bait hits the water facing away from you. Also, when you tug on the line, you turn the bait around facing back toward the sailfish. Although they can still get around back to the boat eventually, the constant flashing and turning interaction going on between you and the baitfish will usually draw a bite from the sailfish.

# Fast Baits

These are baits you will commonly find in deeper water where you are already set up and fishing for sails. Small "bullet" bonitos and tinker mackerel are favorite food items for sailfish. Tinker mackerel can be caught using the same rig as you would for a goggle-eye. When fishing in deeper water and marking lots of bait below the surface, it pays to send a goggle-eye rig down for closer inspection. Fish a tinker just as you would a goggle-eye.

Often seen popping on the surface or jumping from the water, bullet bonito are slightly more complicated to catch and use.

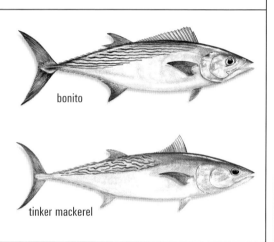

bonito

tinker mackerel

**Bullets are difficult to keep alive in any but the largest livewell. They require a lot of water flow and a large, round tank.**

To catch bullets, you need to troll a string of small feather jigs ahead of a small spoon. A string of these pulled behind a 6- to 12-ounce cigar lead or a small planer is very effective. Bullets are difficult to keep alive in any but the largest livewell. They require a lot of water flow and a large, round tank. If a

bullet doesn't keep swimming, it can't breath and will quickly expire. For this reason you should be ready to catch them and put them out immediately. You must also keep them moving with the boat in gear, once you deploy them as baits. When trolling with bullets, keep the boat moving ahead fast enough to keep your lines straight behind the boat, but not so fast that your baits are up on the surface all the time. Bullets may be one of the most effective yet under-utilized bait choices available to sailfish anglers. A slightly larger bait, bullets should be fished on a

Tiny bonito and mackerel are hard to find and catching them requires trolling with small jigs, but they can be worth the effort. Bonito a little too big are converted into strip baits.

7/0 to 8/0 livebait hook.

Gaining familiarity with the various baits' available is just as important as knowing about the sailfish themselves. Learning the habits of each baitfish species and knowing how to catch them will certainly make you a more successful sailfish angler. You will find that knowing the predator/prey relationship is quite important. Time spent gathering a generous supply of your own bait, with several species in the livewell, can make the difference between catching one or two sailfish and having a double-digit day.

# Live Rigging

U sing live baits around the boat is a surefire method for enticing sailfish. For captains in some regions, it is now the only way they will fish, regardless of cost or time spent catching their own bait. This is especially so in tournaments. Different species are rigged in different ways, to stay shallow or dive deeper, even swim behind a moving boat for miles until a strike happens. Most of this involves simple hook placement, but bridling a bait goes the extra mile.

Shoulder-hooked "greenie" or threadfin herring dives deeper.

## Rigging the Bridle Loop

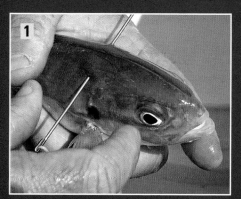

A bridle operates on the idea that sewing floss instead of a hook allows the bait to swim more freely.

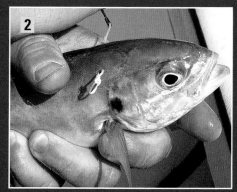

Needle passes through bait with short loop of floss or rubber band attached leaving enough to pass hook through.

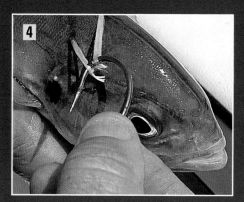

Insert hook through both loops on each end of the floss and then start twisting the hook.

Spin the hook a few times to take up slack, then loop the hook once between bait and floss. It won't unravel.

Nose-hooked baits tend to stay higher in the water.

Tail-hooking pitch baits keeps them pointed away from the boat.

**3**

Needle is detached, leaving a convenient loop on each end of the bait for the hook to slip into.

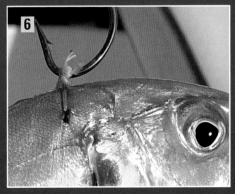

**6**

Locked in place, the hook stays very close to the bait, but far enough away to offer a clean hookup without fouling.

Live bait goes for a swim offshore. Spin reel is kept in free-spool, with a soft copper wire just holding the line from going out— until a big fish strikes.

# CHAPTER 12

# Getting Busy

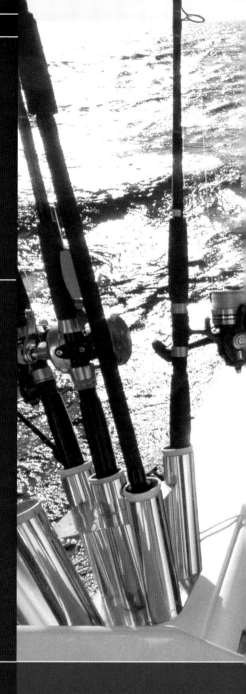

**A**ll systems are go. You've planned your day, acquired bait, selected the right tackle and teasers. Now it's time to put things together. Will you be kite-fishing? If this live-bait specialty is the order of the day, you'll need to know how to use the tools most efficiently. The same goes for deadbait trolling from the outriggers, flatline livebait drifting, running teaser rigs—each method has its own techniques. Then, the strike. The dropback ensures the sailfish has actually taken the bait, and is not just swatting it or cradling it between the jaws. Once you're engaged, a vital dialogue opens between angler and captain. You have to communicate where the fish is heading, how best to maneuever the boat, and whether it's necessary to chase the fish to regain line. So many decisions.

**Lots of techniques to learn in sailfishing. This can get complicated or kept simple.**

Alert crew watches various kite baits for any sign of nervousness. Or a dark blob in the water, which may be armed with a sharp bill.

# Getting Right With the Gear

To give you an idea how a typical day of sailfishing begins, takes place and ends, let's take a look at the sequence of events from start to finish.

## Leaders

Before beginning, you will have your rods already set up to fish with wind-on shock leaders. That's a dual-purpose leader used whether you troll or livebait. Wind-on means you can reel the whole leader through the rod guides and onto the reel. Most veterans start by tying a loop in the end of the main line, making a double line. You can use a Bimini twist, spider hitch, uni-knot or even a simple surgeon's knot to make this loop. Some make the double line as long as six feet, but you really need only a foot or so. The goal is to form the strongest possible connection between your fishing line and shock leader. To the double line you'll attach the leader by tying a line-to-line knot such as an Albright knot or a Yucatan knot. Unless you're a world record hunter and wish to comply with IGFA requirements, spool 30 feet or so of leader material on the reel. You can snell your hook directly to this leader for outrigger or flatline fishing. If you're kite fishing or trolling dead baits, add a snap swivel to the end of this leader. You will then need a selection of shorter (6- to 8-foot) leaders pre-tied for your kite baits, or a cooler full of rigged trolling baits.

There are a few reasons why a long wind-on leader is practical. First, since the last 30 feet or so is often the hardest line to get back on the reel, the extra leader length allows you to get control of a fish while they are still reasonably frisky. This promotes good, healthy releases. Secondly, the extra length gets you back in the game quicker after you release a fish. If you cut away the abraded end of your leader after a 'rigger or flatline fish, simply snell a new hook on the end of the line. You can do this several times before a new wind-on is necessary. With a kite fish, the wind-on seldom is affected. Simply replace the used leader at the snap swivel. With your leaders already made up, it's down with the outriggers and time to fish.

**The extra leader length gets you back in the game quicker after you release a fish.**

A quality leader is critical in a situation like this, when it's wrapped around an abrasive sailfish bill. Long leaders of 30 feet are common here.

Leaders are checked and re-checked, prior to tournament fishing with a sortie at dawn.

Deckhand uses outrigger halyard (in left hand) to angle kite line (overhead) out and away from the transom. This is a good tactic for flybridge sportfishers, on which the fishing space is limited to the stern area. Left, a stainless steel ring has been affixed to the halyard. This yoke carries the kite line.

## Line in the Clips

When you are ready to hang a line up from the outrigger clip, there are two ways to accomplish this. When fishing with dead baits, set the release tension only heavy enough to prevent the wave action or occasional piece of grass on your bait from pulling the clip open.

## Fish lines with a release device, since reels are in freespool.

Send the line straight through the clip so that you can feed the sailfish right out of the outrigger. This is a useful practice for a situation where you have multiple lines being eaten at once. Keeping the lines separated during an attack is preferable to dropping baits back on top of one another. It's also more likely that a fish will feel you pulling line out of the clip and drop the bait. If the fish pulls the line out of the clip on his own, that's fine. For flatlines, you can mount release clips on your transom to hold the lines in place. It's preferable to fish all of the lines out of some type of release device, since you will be fishing the reels in freespool.

It's important to have as little strain on the line as possible at the moment when a sail attacks. Ideally, the fish should not feel resistance once it has the bait. Realize the possibility that a backlash exists, if you don't get to a rod that gets hit, before line starts running off the spool. If fish keep beating you to the rod, you can fish the reels in "heavy freespool" until your eyes get better and you start seeing the fish before they bite. Heavy freespool is accomplished by setting the drag lever balancing on the freespool button, which partially engages the clutch on the reel. This will add only enough resistance to keep the spool from over-running itself.

For livebait fishing, you need to set the line in the clips in a manner that won't allow the baits to constantly be pulling line off the reel. For this job, simply grab the line, forming a

Release clips vary and are designed to pop loose only when a predator fish hits. That's a pin-release spring clip with ceramic ring on a kite line, above. Below is a different style release clip, set up for trolling from an outrigger. Fishing line has been outfitted with hollow Dacron and back-spliced loop, to avoid chafing.

loop at the point where you want to clip it. Make several circles with one hand, while holding both ends of the loop with the other. Insert the end of this twisted loop into the clip and tighten the clip only enough to prevent the bait from opening the clip. This setup requires the sailfish to pull line from the clip before the dropback sequence begins. If you happen to be watching a sail chase the bait around and a bite looks imminent, you can pull the line out gently yourself. The sailfish shouldn't feel this, since you're pulling on the clip only and not down the line past the clip.

**A kite rod and reel are designed for only one purpose, kite fishing. Use a short rod for this tactic and a revolving spool reel.**

## Getting the Kite Up

If you elect to fly a kite, you'll first have to get it in the air. If you have an open boat it's simply a matter of pulling the kite out and attaching it to your kite line and sending it away from the boat. With unobstructed airflow, it's pretty remarkable how steady a kite will fly in the appropriate wind. If you keep the kite you're flying matched to the manufacturer's guideline for wind speed, they seem to just fly straight back and stay there. On the other hand, if you try to fly a heavy wind kite on a light breeze day, you'll be fishing it out of the water before long. It's very important to be consistent here.

On a larger boat with obstructions such as a flying bridge or tower, you need to be a little more careful. Anything that breaks up the wind flow will cause the kite to pitch back and forth and crash. To give the kite an even wind stream and get it started away from the boat, point the boat slightly off center into the wind. From the upwind aft corner of the

bridge you can reach out into the straight wind blowing across your cockpit and send the kite off the rod tip until it gets free of conflicting air currents around the boat. Once the kite is 75 feet or so away, it should just sit there and behave until you are ready to get the bait lines attached. Some big boat skippers attach a stainless ring to the outrigger halyard, and use that to guide the kite up and away from the boat.

A kite rod and reel are designed for only one purpose, kite fishing. Use a short rod designated for this tactic and a revolving spool reel, spooled with braided line or light Dacron. There are a couple of ways to rig your kite release clips into the line. One type of clip is threaded onto the running line, where it stays at a pre-measured distance from the kite and each successive clip. The distance between the clips is maintained by tying a series of barrel swivels into the kite line at 75-foot intervals to measure the space between each clip. The release clips are threaded onto the running line through two holes, which are drilled in successively smaller diameters for each clip on the line. A maximum of three clips for each reel is standard. The barrel swivels are sized in sequence as well. The first swivel on the reel comes out at 75 feet and is small enough to pass through holes on the back two release clips, but not the lead one. This swivel will pick up the outside clip and carry it

Find an uninterrupted flow of wind, before releasing the kite. You don't want it to crash and grow heavy with salt.

See DVD for more on kite fishing techniques.

Helium balloons keep those kites up all day, when the breeze finally dies down.

away from the boat. The next swivel will pass through the back clip but not the middle one. With another 75 feet of line off the reel, away goes clip No. 2. Finally, the last swivel catches the remaining clip and you're finished. Three baits are a lot of baits to manage from a single kite and are not always necessary.

The third clip is useful for fishing a two-bait setup with your kite. If you have a bite on the long kite bait with two baits out, to get anoth-er long bait out you'll either have to reel in the short bait and make it into the long bait before adding a fresh short bait, or simply send the short bait back and make the third clip your new short bait. This is a handy, time-saving trick.

For folks who enjoy simplicity, there are also release clips available that attach anywhere on the kite line you choose—by means of a spring clip. With this clip, you simply send the kite

Kite positioning can vary, depending on wind direction and boat drift. Some boats have at least 20 inset rod holders, so that the crew can constantly re-set rods where they need to be.

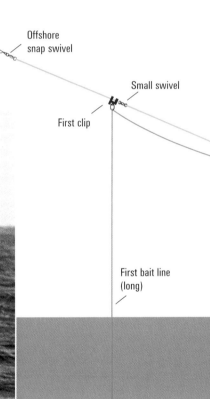

Offshore snap swivel

Small swivel

First clip

First bait line (long)

Whap! Bait under the low kite gets spanked by a sailfish.

Bait hooked through the back

back a bit and when you're ready to attach the bait and clip, you squeeze the end of the spring device and pinch it over the running line, where it stays until you retrieve the line and remove it.

To deploy baits on the kite, once the first line is ready to be sent, hook your bait and clip the fishing line (above the snap swivel) into the release pin, without twisting it like you did on your outrigger lines. (You might prefer to equip the kite lines with something to make them more visible, once they are away from the boat and fishing. Many people have some difficulty seeing the lines in the sunlight and can't keep track of the baits as a result. It's also easy to add a brightly colored cork above the snap swivel. Slide one of these markers onto your mainline before you tie the swivel on and you will have no trouble locating your baits. Different colored corks can be used on each line, which helps identify

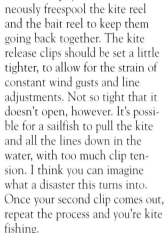

High-vis marker and leader attached to release clip.

which bait is getting attacked by bigger fish.

With the bait in the water and the line secured in the release clip, you must simultaneously freespool the kite reel and the bait reel to keep them going back together. The kite release clips should be set a little tighter, to allow for the strain of constant wind gusts and line adjustments. Not so tight that it doesn't open, however. It's possible for a sailfish to pull the kite and all the lines down in the water, with too much clip tension. I think you can imagine what a disaster this turns into. Once your second clip comes out, repeat the process and you're kite fishing.

You'll notice that the kite rod requires a lot of attention. Ideally, the baits should be splashing around on or just beneath the surface, in an enticing manner. As the wind fluctuates, you'll find the baits are either diving deep or flying 10 feet high. To keep the baits right where you want them, it's easiest to have one person tending the kite rod(s) at all times.

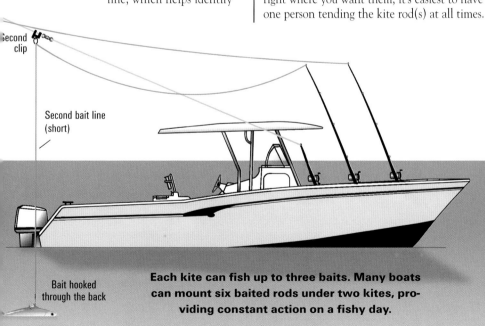

Second clip

Second bait line (short)

Bait hooked through the back

**Each kite can fish up to three baits. Many boats can mount six baited rods under two kites, providing constant action on a fishy day.**

**A sailfish will first appear as a dark blob on the surface. There's no other way to describe it.**

## Waiting for the Bite

Once you have all of your baits positioned, the waiting begins. You may be familiar with a common expression, used to describe offshore big game fishing: "Hours of boredom, interrupted by moments of chaos." I wouldn't disagree with that. It's the watching and analyzing, the adjusting and reacting to different obstacles that make up the balance of your day. This is sailfishing, and the actual hooking and landing of the fish constitutes the smallest part of the total experience. Being completely aware of events leading up to the bite ultimately leads to more time spent catching fish.

While watching your baits, you may have difficulty at first actually seeing the fish in the bait spread. This requires a little practice and experience. Some people have a gift for spotting fish in the water before anyone else. It's possible to train your eyes to pick up anything out of the ordinary. What you should be looking for is any movement or color in the spread, that doesn't blend in with the normal background. Polarized glasses help, of course.

If you spend time staring back at your baits, you'll notice that the water has a definite pattern to it. Not only the color but how the light shines into and beneath it. The sun's reflection on the surface will also have a distinct pattern, which after you watch for a while gets repetitive. When a fish appears in this backdrop, its movement will clash with the rest of the pattern. You are not necessarily looking for a whole fish com-

plete with bill, tail and fins, rather just a shadow or rough outline of the fish. This odd color or shadow moving into the spread will pull your attention. To pick a fish out, watch the entire area behind the boat for irregularities and when that movement happens, you can concentrate more closely and identify the source of attention.

A sailfish will usually appear first as a dark blob below the surface. There is no other way to describe it. I often compare them to seeing a big, plastic trash bag under the spread. The dorsal fin or sail on the fish will be what you see first, if they move in to attack the bait. Many times you'll be watching the spread attentively and "think" you saw this very shadow but after looking back at it, you see nothing else. Pay close attention to the baits when this happens, since very often a fish will be following the baits deeper than you can see and

Keep a finger on the spool with light pressure, if you think a strike is about to happen.

# Run Two Kites

If kite fishing is your preferred method for sailfish, once you've mastered the technique of fishing a single kite without any difficulty, why not push a little harder? Adding a second kite to your arsenal is not as tough as it may sound. You will have to maintain six different lines from a single location, though. This is easily accomplished with the aid of a rocket launcher featuring six rod holders, or a pair of Trident holders located next to each other. This keeps all lines within arm's reach, where you can control length of lines and kites. With two kites flying simultaneously, you're sure to have your hands full when the wind speed is inconsistent. Sudden gusts or lulls in wind speed cause kites to rise and fall constantly. You may find your baits at one moment splashing nervously just below the surface, and just as quickly see them 20 feet in the air, gasping and kicking from an altitude they never dreamed of reaching. For this reason, constant adjustments must be made. It's easiest to assign one person at a time the sole responsibility of tending the kite lines. You can take shifts doing it to break up the routine. After a couple of long days of this exercise, it will become second nature.

To simplify getting two kites to fly together, but not interfere with one another, spread them apart. Begin by adding a little "outboard ballast" to each kite. Simply attach a couple of small split shot leads to the outside corner of the "spar lines" on each kite. This small bit of weight will tilt the kite in the direction of the lead sinker and help steer it off to one side. To get even more separation, once your kite and baits are deployed, clip your kite line into a tagline on your outrigger and send the kite line back via the end of the rigger pole. A tagline is simply a piece of heavy mono or cable snapped to your release clip's swivel, with a large-diameter stainless steel ring at its end. Feed your kite line through the ring before you attach the kite. The ring must be large enough for the release clips to pass through. With the kite deployed, you can send the ring out to the end of the outrigger for more separation. This arrangement frees up the space directly behind the transom for a couple of flatlines or for a deep-run bait. **SB**

Be sure to keep kites apart. They can be run close and far, also high and low, with a minimum of tweaking, including lead weights, below.

See DVD for more on fishing two kites.

return moments later. Usually when you think you saw one, you did. Few things offshore can be mistaken for that dark blob in the water.

## Contact!

Between watching your kite baits splash and the 'rigger clips vibrate, what should you be doing? Watch any professional crew at work and they seem to be one step ahead of the fish. If you expect a bite or you're witnessing one about to happen, the crew should be scrambling before the 'rigger line comes down.

Your designated angler should get to the rod first. Other anglers should also be watching for multiple fish and be prepared to react. With your crew in this position, there usually aren't as many surprises. You're either going to catch one or whiff one, but nobody should be caught off guard.

Assuming a predator fish is after the bait and you've identified which bait is threatened, the angler should be at the proper rod with the reel flipped into freespool. It's wise to leave the rod in the holder until the fish has the bait.

The person at the wheel should be ready to save the location on the GPS where the bite occurred.

Why? A rod you pick up and turn to face the fish with will sometimes get passed up for another bait or two, before the fish commits. The act of switching rods creates confusion. The reel is in freespool: Once the fish takes the bait, remove it from the rod holder. With your thumb gently on the spool to prevent a backlash, point the rod in the direction of the line and let him swim off. Remember to feed the fish through the release clips, if the line

**PRO TIP** JUMPING SAILS

## Free-Jumper Attack

The sight of a free-jumping sailfish builds up your confidence. You know there are fish in the area and that you are close to the bite, when you actually see your target species.

Surprisingly, not many people seem to capitalize on such sightings by going directly to the jumping fish. A jumping sailfish is usually just the tip of the iceberg. Since sails travel together, the odds are pretty good there are more than the one you've just seen.

Watch for free-jumping sailfish; they could mark a pod of fish.

Any time you're running and see a free-jumper, it pays to go directly to the fish and try to cut it off (from its estimated route) with a pitch bait. Watch the direction of travel and speed closely and you can guess where to stop and head off the fish's course. Try to give yourself enough room to slow to a stop and have the bait in the water just as the fish reaches your position. It doesn't have to be done with pinpoint accuracy to work, either. Many times a free-jumper will change course to check out the boat, out of curiosity. The key is to avoid running them over.

If you are already set up fishing and a free-jumper is heading your way, do the same thing. If they are slightly inshore or offshore of the line you've chosen to sit on, ease your way in front of them. If you see repeated jumpers well out of range of your spread, consider relocating to get into the strike zone. Remember, free-jumpers are for catching, not idly watching. **SB**

wasn't twisted for live bait. In kite fishing, there is no need to let the fish swim with the bait; when the line pops out of the release clip, the time it takes for you to wind tight to the fish provides more than ample dropback.

At this point you should know what is going on at the business end of the line. For a sailfish, the process of catching and eating the bait is going to always lead up to one final thing, getting the bait turned headfirst, pointed at their gullet. Now consider the many vari-

there is no set formula or countdown for every situation. The best way to react to any sailfish bite is to wait for the fish to move off steadily with the bait, before getting tight with the line. A sailfish ready to swallow the bait and move on to the next meal will speed up. Waiting for the fish to move off, and locking up when it does, will result in more hookups. This may take three seconds or 30. Just try to read what the fish is doing and react accordingly.

Other situations require a different approach.

## A sailfish ready to swallow the bait and move on to the next meal will speed up. Be ready!

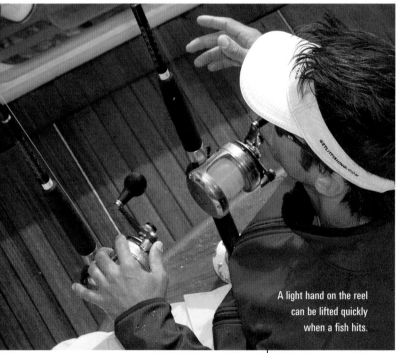

A light hand on the reel can be lifted quickly when a fish hits.

Sometimes a sailfish will eat the bait quickly and have it down the hatch before you ever get to the rod. Other times, a fish will eat the bait and bite down on the hook while the line is in the release clip. This will result in a fish smoking line off the reel or jumping, trying to rid itself of the hook. Any fish that eats like this should be wound tight ASAP. Getting tight on this type of fish may not always result in a caught fish, but it's the only way to get lucky and stick the hook. You can only hope it's somewhere that will hold.

To get back to

ables that will affect the duration of this sequence. Larger baits may require more manipulation. Livelier baits must be killed before the sailfish relaxes its grip and turns them around for swallowing. Some bait might be caught only by the tail and held for a while. Another may quickly end up halfway down the hatch facing the right direction, ready for a quick swallow.

The point is that every bite is different and

the original bite, let the fish take line or even help the line off the reel to reduce tension the fish may feel. You may feel the fish chomping on the bait or you may feel it just sitting there. Try to maintain some contact with the fish if the line gets light. A fish that eats the bait and swims toward you may not seem to be there. This may allow the fish to swallow the bait, which we certainly don't want to happen. At the moment the fish starts to move steadily

Happy campers with big Pacific sailfish, after a successful hookup.

Never freeze up, but follow a hooked fish wherever it goes. On a big boat, that can be more difficult. The captain has to maneuver the boat accordingly.

away, you should push the drag up to strike and with the rod pointed at the line, reel as fast as you can. Don't stop reeling until the drag starts slipping off the reel or you see your bare hook skipping toward the boat.

Whether you fish with circle or J-hooks, you should try to hook the fish with the reel and not the rod. After the line is stretched tight and the drag is peeling line off the reel, you can raise the rod and bend it. When you wind the fish onto the hook, a gradual steady

increase in pressure will move the leader and hook into the corner of the sailfish's jaw. Jerking on slack line often causes the hook to land in the roof of the mouth or grab a piece of skin inside the mouth, which pulls free as soon as pressure is applied.

At this point you should be fast to a wildly jumping sailfish. Never freeze up: The angler should stay with the fish, following it around the cockpit wherever it goes. On a center console boat, that's easier. On a big boat with

fish goes and make room on that side of the boat. If the fish runs directly astern, fine. Wait until he heads off to port or starboard and turn the bow in that direction. You can then move the baits on that side of the boat to the other side, or leave them close to the boat on stand-by if necessary.

The point is to keep fishing. Sailfish often travel in groups and the fact you finally crossed paths with them should be taken advantage of. Tripleheaders and quads sometimes bite one at a time, so don't get antsy to move. Be prepared to grab a pitch rod, to get extra baits to fish that get past your spread.

If you get in over your head and find it necessary to clear lines and run a fish down with the boat, so be it. In the event this happens, use your GPS to get back to the spot pronto where the bite began and reload. On the other hand, if everything's going smoothly and you

Hard fighter in choppy seas. These fish can be caught on fairly small reels for offshore fish.

stern cockpit, the captain has to keep the fish from getting under the boat—by moving the boat. The rest of your crew should be ready for another bite. Never be in a hurry to clear all of your lines and go after a hooked fish. Sailfish will seldom "dump" an entire reel and usually settle down fairly quickly. Try not to disturb the rest of your bait spread until it's absolutely necessary. Ideally, you should turn in the direction the

can wait for more bites while fighting that one fish, by all means do so.

A few points to consider when fighting a fish: Always stay tight to the fish. Sails have a tendency to run toward you as much as away. You may think the fish got off the hook when this happens, but you can't be sure until you see the end of the line. Always reel fast when your line goes slack. Another trick used when a fish is going to jump—be ready to ease up on the line a little. Watch the angle closely where your line enters the water. When a fish comes up to jump, the line will start angling to the surface. As you see this happening, be prepared to lower the rodtip quickly and reach out toward the fish. It's called "bowing to the fish." This will take a bit of strain off the line while the fish shakes its head. It helps prevent too much pressure that may pull the hook or break the line.

If you find yourself with more than one fish on, always try to release the easy one first. A

fish that stays close to the boat is often easier to get to. The leader can be cut quickly, close to the fish, without disturbing the rest of your spread. To avoid confusion, designate one person to direct the anglers. This is usually done best by the helmsman, since they're looking at the whole picture and can usually see which line is most critical to deal with. Three different people shouting directions can turn into a mess in a heartbeat. In the event you do get two lines crossed or wrapped, back off lightly on the reel drags and put both rodtips together. That makes it easier to determine which way the twist runs. It also eases line friction.

Before you have a fish too close to the boat,

Action on deck! Lines have been pulled in, while a crew member cranks hard on sailfish.

you'll want to get your dredges and teasers out of the way. Teasers fished from the outriggers can be wound up to the point where they're just touching the surface of the water. If you still have a short line in the water, which might get in the way, drop it back away from the boat rather than removing it. This takes less time and leaves an extra line out; you should always be looking for that next bite.

## Boat-Side

At the point where you have the leader out of the water, it's wise to cut the leader near the fish as quickly as possible. More damage is usually done to a fish after the mate takes control of the leader, than at any other time in the fight. Since you are not giving the fish any slack, the hook will exert a greater amount of force on the fish. You did your best not to hook the fish too deeply but invariably there are times when you still gut-hook one. The fish will probably struggle quite a bit more, once it feels it's lost control of its predicament. That's when fatal damage can occur at this stage of the fight. You might see the fish bleeding at the side of the boat. That's when you really should let it go quickly.

That's also the time to decide whether you tag the fish. A tag should be placed in the fish as quickly and efficiently as possible.

If you are compelled to get a photo of the fish, which is perfectly acceptable, be sure your photographer is ready with the camera before the fish is at the boat. The extra time it takes to find the camera and get everyone in position can cost the fish its life. Decide which side of the boat will be best for photos and try to land the fish on that side. Preferably, the fish should be in a position where the sun is over the

Don't pull too hard on the leader. Take just a few extra moments to avoid ripping something on the fish.

cameraman's back, to prevent backlighting. This also will enhance the appearance of the fish in the shot and makes for a more desirable photo.

Lifting a sailfish from the water can also open up another possibility for injury to the fish. In addition to internal injuries to the fish's organs, excessive struggling against the hard boat surface can cause greater injury. If you decide to do this, take care to protect the fish. Be sure to support the fish from underneath.

If you land a fish that is absolutely whipped, it's a good idea to take control of the fish and spend some time reviving it. To capture a fish by the bill and hold it in the water takes some delicate handling, however. This is not only for the fish's, but also for the mate's protection. To bill a fish properly, always grab the bill close to the mouth. Grabbing a sailfish bill near the tip can result in a broken bill, especially in smaller fish. Young sailfish have a very soft, almost rubbery bill that will break easily. Any time you grab a billfish, it's best to hold it with both

## Have the captain turn slightly toward the fish to prevent it from sliding under the boat.

hands. Keep your palms facing down and your thumbs held together. Holding the fish in this manner gives you absolute control and steers the business end of the fish away from yourself and the boat's paint job. It's easily possible for a 50-pound fish to inflict serious injury to a grown man, if he were to get stuck by the fish's bill. You should also be wearing your gloves for this move. A sailfish bill is similar to a coarse steel file and will remove several layers of skin from wet hands if you're not careful. A solid grip on the bill is imperative. One mate from Galveston fishing Cozumel was smacked in the face by a sailfish, leaving a permanent scar that earned him the fond nickname, "Monster."

To revive the fish, once you have control of it, hold the fish in the water and move the boat ahead slowly. Have the captain turn slightly toward the fish to prevent it from sliding under the boat. Keep the fish in the water so that the flow will pass through its mouth and revive the fish's oxygen supply. You should notice the fish becoming more energetic and see some color returning, as well. A really tired fish will take on a dark coppery color and as it gets its strength back, this color will change back to normal. As soon as the fish has its tail wagging back and forth and it appears to be swimming along with you, or it simply starts to struggle to get free, take the boat engines out of gear and let it go.

You'll often hear stories of fish that were brought back to the dock because they "came up dead" or couldn't be revived. I can tell you from personal experience this really happens only rarely. Of the thousands of sailfish landed on my boat over the years, very few were brought in beyond the point of saving. The exception to this has always been a foul-hooked fish that took too long to

Reviving a sailfish by dragging it forward through the water.

catch, or a tail-wrapped fish that came in backwards—and died from being pulled backwards. I have seen many sailfish that appeared beyond saving, only to come back and swim away in good shape. This sometimes requires lost fishing time, but it's certainly worth it in the long run. Don't be afraid to take 15 minutes to drag a tired fish around, if it will save the fish. Remember, you may catch it again someday. It's happened before.

## Back in the Game

After the high-fives are done and everyone is full of adrenaline, don't waste time getting back in the action. If you're still in position and have baits in the water, get your spread back out as quickly as possible and get ready for the next round of action. If the fish took you out of

ally made up of a couple of great flurries of activity, with a lot of waiting in between. It's rare that the bites are spaced out evenly throughout the day. For this reason, strike while the iron is hot! Working together efficiently as a team with friends and enjoying the chance to tangle with such a magnificent animal with people who appreciate the day is what it's all about. Giving everyone on the boat a chance to catch one on the same day is something to strive for. But you have to take advantage of every opportunity, to achieve this goal. **SB**

A fine day spent offshore. A returning fleet proudly raises sailfish release flags before docking again.

## Numbers

A final thought on the numbers game is in order. If you practice the tactics outlined in these pages, you should increase your catch rates before too long. One of the best parts of any recreational activity is learning the game, improving your ability and mastering it. Something that happens to a lot of anglers (and it's unfortunate) is the fact they measure their success or failure based on another angler's performance. Try to remember the reason you're out there when you take off to spend a day on the water. You should never go out with the expectation you're going to catch more fish than everyone else. In a tournament this wouldn't be the case, of course. Even in a competitive setting, don't allow your standing on the leader board to get in the way of having fun.

I've seen too many anglers go out and have their best personal day ever sailfishing, then return to the dock, only to wilt when they found out someone else caught a few more than they did. Always go out and give it your best shot, and be happy you just spent the day offshore, pursuing something you love. The chance to battle fish and burn up a few days on blue water should be reward enough. Go into this sport with that attitude and you'll eventually have a day where you're the high-liner (high-scoring boat) and you might not even notice. Either way, you'll have fun doing it. **SB**

position or too far away from where the bite happened, get back as soon as you can. Remember that sailfishing action happens fast. Bites often go off in flurries and if you miss time when these fish have decided to feed, you'll never catch as many as you could have.

A typical day where you end up with 10 or 15 releases is usu-

# CHAPTER 13

# Q&A
## With a
## Tournament Pro

Ovi Verona

**W**hat follows is a casual interview with Miami's Capt. Ray Rosher and some of his talented crew members, after a successful string of tournament victories in South Florida and two consecutive wins in Baja, California. Keeping ahead of a pack of talented boat crews requires a team that runs like a fine Swiss watch.

Motivation, talent, experience, a willingness to follow orders, a smooth plan of attack, lack of panic with multiple sailfish hooked up, thinking ahead before that next fish is even released. It also doesn't hurt that everyone aboard knows how to perform each other's job, including driving the boat. Redundant systems, if you will.

## Words from a hot tournament captain with the perfect fishing crew.

DVD SPECIAL FEATURE: Exclusive interview with Capt. Ray Rosher and the "Get Lit" team.

A shotgun start in a South Florida sailfish tournament means a great variety of watercraft sprinting up and down the coast—because sailfish are caught so close to the beach. If kayaks can catch sailfish, all of these vessels are more than eligible.

# Talent, Practice, a Sixth Sense

There's nothing more valuable than a trusted fish report. Most people in tourneys are honest and we all try to help each other. We have to be happy with other's success too. You have to help others like you've been helped. A lot of success has come from others when we were struggling. Networking is a two-way street. You have to get and give honest answers.

I n the year leading up to this sailfish book going to press, Capt. Ray Rosher in Miami was the hottest sailfish tournament skipper in Florida, racking up huge numbers of releases and setting records. His crew's total of 59 sailfish in one January tournament, that lasted 2.5 days, raised eyebrows in surrounding coastal states. *Florida Sportsman* had cameras on board that day, and photos from that trip are scattered throughout this book. We felt that anglers would be curious about Ray's approach to sailfishing, and so we interviewed him afterwards. We've cleaned up the conversation some here, for brevity's sake.

Captain Ray Rosher heading offshore.

**LaBonte:** When a captain wins as many tournaments as you have, there's a lot going on. We know there are many aspects that go into the whole picture, so let's take it apart one at a time, starting with locations. What are you looking for, offshore?

**Rosher:** We look for the most in (good) conditions and that changes by the hour. You'll start in one area and conditions can improve or disintegrate. The hard part is knowing when to say "enough." Sometimes you're better off being patient. Knowing when to be patient and when to be aggressive is a very difficult decision.

**LaBonte:** If you know there's fish in the area and if you have faith in the spot, you'll camp out and wait for them to begin feeding?

**Rosher:** Sometimes. There are a lot of other factors that can make you move. Finding information from a trusted source, for instance.

**LaBonte:** The actual signs—current, moving water, bait in the area and fish there, that's when you know you're in the right place? You try to put as many of these factors together in one location?

**Rosher:** Absolutely. All those things you mentioned are very important. Fish will throw curve balls, though. I've seen great conditions and no bites. And bad conditions with bites. One day the guys wanted food fish, so we sat for kingfish and tuna, but by the end of the day, you realize it's been a banner day for sailfish. The next day, we're excited, get extra bait and end up 0 for 1 on sailfish. As soon as you think you have it figured out, it changes.

*Get Lit* backing down fast on a speedy sailfish. Kitt Toomey winds the fish while crew members are already prepping more live baits for the kites.

## "If you have good bait and handle it well, it will live in your livewell. The more you handle them, the more bacteria attacks."

**LaBonte:** Let's talk about bait. That's a critical factor, especially in tournaments. You can't be worrying about your bait. In South Florida the price of bait is an issue, too. It can get costly, and people limit themselves to what they can afford. You guys keep an ample amount of bait. Do you take the time to catch your own bait all the time?

**Rosher:** We try to always have bait purchased for the tourney. I have a little bait business myself. The bottom line is, we're not out catching goggle-eyes [which requires night fishing]. We buy goggle-eyes, but we catch other species. You need to go catch bait a day or two ahead of the tourney and handle them [the bait] well. The bottom line is, if you have good bait and handle it well, it will live in

your livewell. The more you move your bait, the more you handle [them], the more bacteria attacks.

**LaBonte:** When you dig [around] in your well for baits, you're doing a lot of extra handling.

**Rosher:** Pay attention; don't take giant scoops [with the net]. Just go for the one you want.

**LaBonte:** Tell me a little about catching bait while you fish out there. Is that something you do?

**Rosher:** A little bit. When we mark bait, some tourneys allow it [and] some don't. If you can drop a sabiki rig in baitfish while you sailfish, it does a couple of things. First, it replenishes your supply with hot, fresh baits. Second, it can sometimes bring sailfish up...

Hooked sailfish tailwalks suddenly, while more lines are readied for the water.

**LaBonte:** Raising fish, bringing the school up. We get that in Jupiter where I fish. It will often trigger a bite, especially when the baitfish get nervous, and they're holding tight. If you can break that bunch up...

**LaBonte:** You have a saying that you use, can you share that?

**Rosher:** It's my wife's favorite, "It's all about the math."

**LaBonte:** Tell me what you mean by that.

**Rosher:** Everyday, there are many things that pertain to efficiency. It's all about catch ratio, how long it takes to deploy baits, keeping baits in the water longer. The more exposure you have of baits to sailfish, the greater your shot. I always think from the tower, "If we would have taken another minute, or stumbled, we would have missed it."

**LaBonte:** We saw it in the video, your guys were all ready to go before it was time for lines in the water. You had a sailfish hooked up within minutes. You must have caught the first fish that day. You were parked where you had confidence, and your guys and wife had your gear ready to go. If you had taken your time, that fish probably would have gone by and been missed. You want to maximize your time, have baits in the water as long as possible, That's part of your strategy?

**Rosher:** Many times, if we're hooked up, the other guy who's not busy is up on the bow. I like nothing more than to hear (from the bow), "I'm on!" It makes me look great, and I didn't do anything.

**LaBonte:** Speaking of guys on the bow, you have guys up there catching fish?

**Rosher:** We put four rod holders on the bow. [Owner] Kitt doesn't mind if we cut holes in his boat.

**LaBonte:** Let's talk a little about the Silver Sailfish Derby. In 2006 they set a record for sailfish caught and you guys had first place. There were 2.5 days of fishing and 958 sails caught by only 50 boats. Get Lit caught 59 sailfish to win the event...incredible.

**Rosher:** It was an honor to be a part of that. It may never happen again in our lifetimes.

**LaBonte:** We were fortunate to have some cameras on your boat that day. Did you have an idea that something special was happening?

**Rosher:** By about 10 a.m. you realize your numbers are climbing and conditions are right. One time during the day, we had a pack of fish come through. For whatever reason we didn't capitalize on them. In the right situation, if you miss a couple, you can run back ahead and set up in front of them. I had a little gap in the other boats south of me, where they were running. A lot of times you can keep your kites out, [move the boat a little] and swing them into position. When I'm [moving and] running, my guys will have the long baits clipped in, but in the baitwell. We ended up [that day] with two kites [crashed] in the water. From that point on, I said we're not going to get fancy, there were more fish coming, so by 10 o'clock, you realize it's a special day. You don't need to do anything fancy, just keep baits in the water. We were fishing in 120 to 140 feet. Kitt and Pete both have a great eye for sailfish from a low vantage point [on deck]. They point them out to me. I remember one time we were fighting a fish and saw tailers out farther offshore. If you're fishing a small swath of water, and you see fish out deeper, you wonder how many fish went by you that day.

**Labonte:** Tell us about a tailing fish. Visually trying to look for the fish itself. They're not very visible like that. A tailer is

kind of a grayish, blue drab color that blends in with the water. Are you constantly looking for them when you're fishing?

**Rosher:** We try. As many times as possible we'll have an extra person in the tower, just to look around. If I don't have that luxury, the crew is looking at our baits out there. If I see some tailers and get a bite out of them, I feel like I've done something that day.

**LaBonte:** What about free-jumpers? Is that something you chase after? A tailer can turn into a free-jumper just like that, and a lot of people think you can't catch them.

**Rosher:** A free-jumper is a fish that may be jumping for a variety of reasons. It signifies to us the tip of the iceberg. There can be 5 to 10 fish, but you only see one free-jumper. If you can put your spread in front of them, there's no telling what will happen. I've seen as many as 15 sailfish in one pack.

**Rosher:** My favorite conditions for sailfishing are whatever causes them to bite. I've seen

Neutral tournament observer watches a bow-hooked fish aboard *Get Lit,* during a cold weather tournament.

almost all conditions yield bites, and I've seen those same conditions yield no bites. On the average, the best shot you have is a tailing condition and/or with a north current in our area. They like to swim into the current, like trout in a river. They want to face the current to bring them food. If you get wind going against the current, it facilitates that process. They can surf down the face of the waves, fins folded back, almost like wolves, sliding along silently. Bait comes by and they flare up and eat it. It's a neat process to watch.

**LaBonte:** Talk about some of your favorite techniques offshore.

**Rosher:** We fish for sails with a lot of different methods. I enjoy kite fishing, the ability to lift baits up and let a fish pass by. With rigger fishing, you have to wind in baits if they tangle or it can turn into a mess. Kites allow you to be more efficient. Simple is also great. During charters we pitch baits and have a few flatlines out on a calm day. Seeing sailfish chase pilchards before they get to you is pretty fun.

**Rosher:** Now we're here with four-fifths of our team. John Cooper is in The Bahamas today. We have Kitt Toomey, owner extraordinaire and quietest guy on the team. Peter Miller, the crusher, and my wife Charmain Rosher. It's a pleasure to fish with the team and makes my job very easy.

**LaBonte:** Tell me how important it is to have a team that works well together.

**Rosher:** One thing we always talk about, is that it's not important how we approach something, it's important we all approach it the same way. A good example is getting hooked up with a fish going into the wind. We'll fight a lot of fish from the bow. We don't talk much about it, but they see which way the boat's moving. If Kitt's hooked on the left side and going into the wind, someone will move the kite rod. Then someone will jump on the gunnel, so Kitt doesn't have to be awkward while fighting it. We just start chugging along after the fish.

> **"The most exciting thing about sailfishing is getting the initial bite. Kitt is usually watching three baits, and I'm watching three. The moment where it just erupts is second to none."**

**LaBonte:** You'll stay in the cockpit if you can, but you don't hesitate to send someone up to the bow?

**Rosher:** That's the easiest way to fight one. It takes the right fish. If the fish goes cross-sea, that's not the fish to do it with. We've discussed all that beforehand and we're on the same page. In short, we've had great success fishing on the bow. If it's a four-line tourney, and we have three fish on, we go up to the bow and try for a fourth. It gets crowded. It's the greatest feeling; it's like a free fish up there.

**Peter Miller:** That's the most rewarding fish, when you have a multiple on, and you're watching your last bait, and you get a bite on that one. It's wrapped around the bow, you can barely see the cork, you feel the pressure, and you get a quad on. It's exciting when you can barely see it, barely feel it and everyone's on a fish.

**Rosher:** I personally look at each fish as being unique. There are so many situations, so many techniques, kite fishing, flatlines, weighted lines, balloons. A myriad of ways to catch fish and they all bring their own challenge and excitement. I'm not tired of seeing sailfish yet.

**Miller:** We've all been fishing our entire lives. Every sailfish is different. Each is exciting. First bend in the rod, we all watch each other. Even if I'm winding on my fish, I'm watching Kitt's. Ray is watching from above. Every time it's exciting and spectacular. None of us has ever lost that excitement for fishing. Every bite is worth it.

**Toomey:** Each day you don't know what you're going to get. We've seen so many interesting things sailfishing, had swords and blue marlin come up in our spreads. When you're out there, you see so much, even whales. So often you see something you haven't seen before. It makes each day exciting.

**Miller:** The most exciting thing about sailfishing is getting the initial bite. Kitt is usually watching three baits, and I'm watching three. The moment where it just erupts is second to none. You may get three, four or five bites. In the Silver Derby we had three sailfish going after one bait, bouncing off one another trying to eat it. It was spectacular and gets my adrenaline through the roof.

**Rosher:** Like I said about that day, I wish everybody could see what I'm seeing. I saw so many spectacular bites in one day, I was blown away by the end of that day. How many times did we see things like Pete was saying. I wish I could have it all recorded, but you just have to carry those memories in your mind, and that's what keeps you coming back.

**LaBonte:** Aside from the fact that we're in a big tournament boat, we still call it blue-collar billfishing. They're here right off our coast and available to just about anybody. It's possible to catch them from a pier, kayaks, even the beach. I think that's a big part of what makes them really cool, billfish for the everyday guy.

**Rosher:** We had a guy a couple of days ago during a charter who approached us in a 17-foot skiff. He bummed half a dozen baits and we watched him catch a sailfish. There's not a blue marlin alive that would have made this guy happier. He took pictures and released it. He was jumping up and down on a 17-foot skiff. So it's really rewarding, a special fish and we're privileged to catch them.

Reviving sailfish by dragging them along through the water.

**LaBonte:** Tell me a little about your tackle. There's a lot of hooks and leaders. Is there some sort of guideline of where you're at with this?

**Rosher:** We fish all Penn 16VS reels with 20-pound test for the tourneys. All Berkley leader and line. We fish a variety of hooks based on the tournament. During the Silver Derby in Palm Beach, we had to use the Penn P170 and the Eagle Claw 2004 circle hooks. I always use circle hooks now. If you're attentive to the bite, you don't experience many bleeding fish. You can gut-hook them on both circles and J-hooks. Here was my aversion to circle hooks early on: they were allowed to have 5-degree offsets.

More fish were bleeding with those than my J-hooks at the time. I tried not to say anything, but I did not see enough jaw-hooked fish at the time. Then they changed the rule to zero-offset circle hooks, and I now believe the fish don't suffer as much mortality as a J-hooked fish. Part of the reason is that the point is now 270 degrees. If it does perforate the stomach, it doesn't damage other organs.

John Cooper, Carlos Garcia, Kitt Toomey, Charmain and Ray Rosher, and Peter Miller released 59 sailfish in the 2006 Palm Beach Silver Derby.

This season, a sailfish was killed on a dock near me. They filleted the fish and it had three circle hooks in its stomach lining. It was caught with a fourth hook, so what that tells you, is that the fish can survive with three hooks in him. Who knows if they were offset? That fish survived three catches and had a fourth. We tagged and released a sail off Haulover in April in North Miami, and caught it 6 months later, 20 miles south of there. That tells you these fish are not as migratory as once thought. There were plenty of north winds in that 6-month period and the fish only moved 20 miles. It tells you that this conservation method of using circle hooks does matter.

**LaBonte:** Just a quick thought on taking care of the boat. Making sure the boat is right, about having everything dealt with before-hand, so there are no surprises.

**Rosher:** Obviously, keeping the boat in good repair is important. Keep a handle on things and everything working, having back-ups like even a kite reel; we have a spare rigged and ready to go. Backup conventional rods and spinners. If you fray a line, we just pop the reel off. I number or color-code my rods. I like colors, because I can't read the numbers from up in the tower. If we have lines cross, I can look down and reinforce that the red and the green came together. After we get the fish, we know which rod to replace.

**LaBonte:** I notice you guys have extra rods ready to go. That allows you to keep baits in the water more.

**Rosher:** We love to run out of rods. Pete and Froggy are really good at re-rigging quick-ly. That helps a lot. We all have our jobs, but overall everybody can do each other's jobs. Any of these guys can run the boat. It helps them understand. When I'm charter fishing, my mates become better by running the boat for a day. Efficiency getting the bait in front of the fish is important. When you run the boat one day, and the fish goes past the bow and is gone, it makes them quicker in the cockpit. Good livewells—I can't say enough about good livewells on the boat. We have a couple of pump boxes. You can back down as much as you want [into the wake and bubbles without stalling the pumps with air pockets]. I've fished a lot of tourneys, where on a rough day, people lose their entire load of bait in the livewells.

**LaBonte:** That's a mood killer.
**Rosher:** Not good.
**Rosher:** You mentioned earlier about get-ting enough sleep before tournaments. Fortunately, Kitt and everybody on the team have at one time or another attended the captains' meeting while the rest of us get bait prepped, or vice versa. Everybody helps each other out. The night before the tournament, we all try to get a good night's sleep. There's very little beer consumed on this boat. The most ironic part of this whole team is that despite the name, *Get Lit* is probably the driest boat in the fleet. **SB**

# CHAPTER 14

# Destination Sailfish

Here is a breakdown of sailfish hotspots in the Southeastern United States and Caribbean region, where most angler effort can be found in clusters. This happens because dependable numbers of sailfish are available just offshore. After all, you won't find an entire fleet of sailfish anglers based where few fish are around. Because these fish are so widespread, we've included maps for easy visualization.

If you really want a shot at having a multiple sailfish day, whether as visiting tourist or re-locating near the coast, you simply can't beat these segments of our coastline. Though sails can be found almost anywhere, you will certainly improve your odds greatly by concentrating in these areas at the right time of year, when they're passing through in great numbers.

**Narrowing the search, in a quest for sailfish hookups.**

If you follow the migrations, it's possible to stay with sailfish all year long. You would have to jump from Sailfish Alley in South Florida in winter, to the Yucatan in Mexico for spring, up to North Carolina for the summer, then follow the fish through South Carolina down to Cape Canaveral during autumn.

# Starting the Sailfish Search

Sailfish may range across much of the world's tropical oceans but nowhere are they more targeted than in the southeastern United States. That's because of their proximity to so many anglers, who now have the means to pursue these fish. From the Outer Banks of North Carolina to Texas and the Mexican Yucatan, this huge stretch of water is home to Atlantic sailfish. This segment of the world's sailfish population undoubtedly has the greatest economic impact and subsequent value as a sport resource.

These particular fish cover a

**Each summer, anglers from Wrightsville Beach to Oregon Inlet enjoy outstanding sailfish opportunities.**

great deal of water in their lifetime and their seasonal migrations are easy to follow. While this is a huge piece of offshore real estate to choose a fishing hole, certain areas do stand out. If your home waters are anywhere near these hotspots, or you plan to visit, you have a good chance of running into sailfish. Let's get a better idea of when and where that meeting will take place.

## Outer Banks/North Carolina

During the warm summer months, anglers from Wrightsville Beach to Oregon Inlet enjoy outstanding sailfish opportunities. Blue water off North Carolina has a lucky feature that makes this one of the premier offshore destina-

tions. This is where the Gulf Stream again moves close to land—and anglers get a crack at fish that have been far offshore, rested for quite some time. Lack of human interaction helps make these fish willing participants, whenever a spread of natural baits goes bouncing by.

The relatively long distance to the Gulf Stream south of North Carolina (as in South Carolina and upper Georgia) keeps sailfish far offshore of most fishermen for a time. This is a powerful draw for anglers from around the country, who fish out of North Carolina.

North Carolina boat backing down on a fish offshore. Here, sails mix with marlin.

When sailfish arrive off North Carolina in early summer, they've endured a long winter while traveling and playing tag-and-release with Florida anglers. The long swim from Florida gives these fish a chance to ride the current north and recharge their batteries, so to speak. When they arrive in North Carolina, they're usually very aggressive.

Anglers targeting them will find these fish extremely cooperative along the edge of the dropoff and east into the edge of the Gulf Stream. This is a trolling bite primarily and

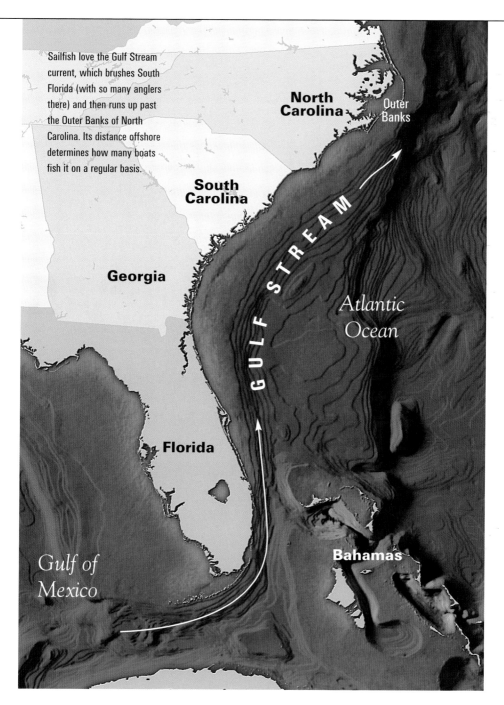

Sailfish love the Gulf Stream current, which brushes South Florida (with so many anglers there) and then runs up past the Outer Banks of North Carolina. Its distance offshore determines how many boats fish it on a regular basis.

North Carolina

Outer Banks

South Carolina

Georgia

GULF STREAM

Atlantic Ocean

Florida

Gulf of Mexico

Bahamas

while you're busy fighting off hits from dolphin, tuna and wahoo, expect frequent visits from sailfish and white marlin. While the blue marlin fishery here is also exceptional and heavier tackle is the norm, mix some smaller baits into your spread and use lighter tackle to take advantage of the plentiful sailfish action that goes with this territory.

## South Carolina-North Florida

This stretch of ocean, while not as accessible, is not entirely ignored by offshore anglers.

Migrating sailfish feels the hook and tailwalks, a great crowd-pleaser.

## This part of Florida seems to be a staging area for sailfish getting ready to invade the famed "Sailfish Alley" farther south.

Migrating sailfish are targeted here, as well, by anglers willing to travel the greater distance necessary to reach them. Fortunately, these sailfish are found during a period of fairly predictable weather patterns. A run of 30 to 60 miles offshore is possible for even small craft here, when fair weather and calm seas of late spring and early fall arrive. So, anglers here get two shots annually at these fish as they travel past.

In the early season, sailfish migrate north and may be scattered over a larger portion of the edge. These early summer fish are both moving and spawning. This behavior spreads them out and they don't seem to be in any particular hurry to be anywhere. They can be found closer to the beach at this time of year, as well, since water temperatures are stable and ample bait supplies keep them around a bit longer in the nearshore areas. Since they're more scattered, it can make finding them more of a challenge as well. Most encounters with sailfish at this time of year are by chance, with anglers targeting other fish such as kingfish.

On their return trip south in the fall, sailfish are more single-minded. These fish are moving south to escape falling water temperatures and will be found in larger concentrations. The mass exodus to warmer climates keeps these fish moving and most of them will be grouped together along the edge, farther offshore. The upside of this is that once the fish are located, you may have multiple shots at them in the same area that day. Another plus in this part of their range is the relatively light fishing pressure they receive, that far offshore.

## Central Florida/ Space Coast

During the fall this can be an exciting place to fish. The winter migration is well under way by October and large numbers of sailfish are on the way to

their wintering grounds farther south. That makes this one of the finest places to enjoy double-digit releases while trolling dead bait. This part of Florida seems to be something of a staging area for fish getting ready to invade the famed "Sailfish Alley" farther south.

As sailfish cruise this area, they encounter more stable water temperatures and plenty of baitfish. The sense of urgency to head south is put on hold temporarily. These fish are found in large schools, feeding on abundant migrating bait schools, which share the same route. The waters between Daytona Beach and Cape Canaveral become a temporary home for a huge concentration of sailfish. Trolling boats who find the bait schools here can get into a

Backing down hard on a fish. It certainly gets exciting at times.

period of deadbait trolling that can rival anywhere in the world. Time it right and a sharp crew can expect a realistic shot at getting well into double digit releases. October and November is when you want to be here. Anglers to the south, fishing in the first deadbait tournaments of the year, have been known to run 50 to 100 miles north to these waters looking for the advantage.

The duration of this bite is largely dependant on the weather. A mild winter and lack of severe early cold fronts can stretch this fishery well into December. This is a great area to get into the action with sailfish—before they run a narrow gauntlet through a great number of South Florida boats with lots of ability. The next few months for these fish are sure to be filled with lots of human interaction. Meeting up with these fish before South Florida boat pressure changes their eating habits can be very rewarding.

## Florida Keys

This is an area where sailfish action can also be fast and furious. The tropical setting of the Keys is a unique backdrop in the U.S. for sailfish anglers. Anglers fishing just off the reef here, about six miles offshore, have an outstanding fishery throughout the winter. While traditional livebait spreads in blue water are very productive, two unique scenarios found in the Keys provide exciting opportunities for anglers. The first involves fishing along the color change after a hard blow stirs up the sandy bottom inshore. White powdery silt stirred up by the wind changes the inshore water from a clear aqua to an opaque powder blue color. Where this water meets the clear cobalt blue water on the edge turns into a barrier line that sailfish love to cruise along. This distinct edge will concentrate bait and fish alike. Setting up on this

**The tropical setting of the Keys is a unique backdrop in the U.S. for sailfish anglers. They fish right off the reef here.**

edge or cruising along its length can be phenomenal.

The second scenario involves full contact fish over the shallower reefs. Sailfish often cruise the inshore reefs, terrorizing pilchards and ballyhoo. When they get into the ballyhoo and "shower" schools of them, the fishing can be hard to beat. Cruising along the reefs, searching for bait showers and frigatebirds diving, is part hunting and part fishing. Getting ahead of the fish and sight-casting live baits is serious medicine for adrenaline junkies.

Winter weather here is often fabulous, mostly sunny and balmy, much better than the rest of the country on average. When sailfish begin cruising over the sand flats in 20 feet of water, where they can be spotted 10 or 15 feet down and cast to—that's quite a kick, as well.

Alligator Light off Islamorada is a great place for rounding up live bait. Just off the reef, ballyhoo shower while sailfish chase them. Is that the sickle fin of a sailfish at bottom left?

# Sailfish Alley December through February is

This stretch of water was once narrowly defined as the area between Stuart and Palm Beach in Southeast Florida. After considerable hours out there, anglers now widely accept that the alley really exists from Fort Pierce to Miami. This is the center of the world's Atlantic sailfish activity, with by far the most angler effort expended to catch them. Sailfish also hang around this stretch of coast on a year-round basis, which is hard to beat.

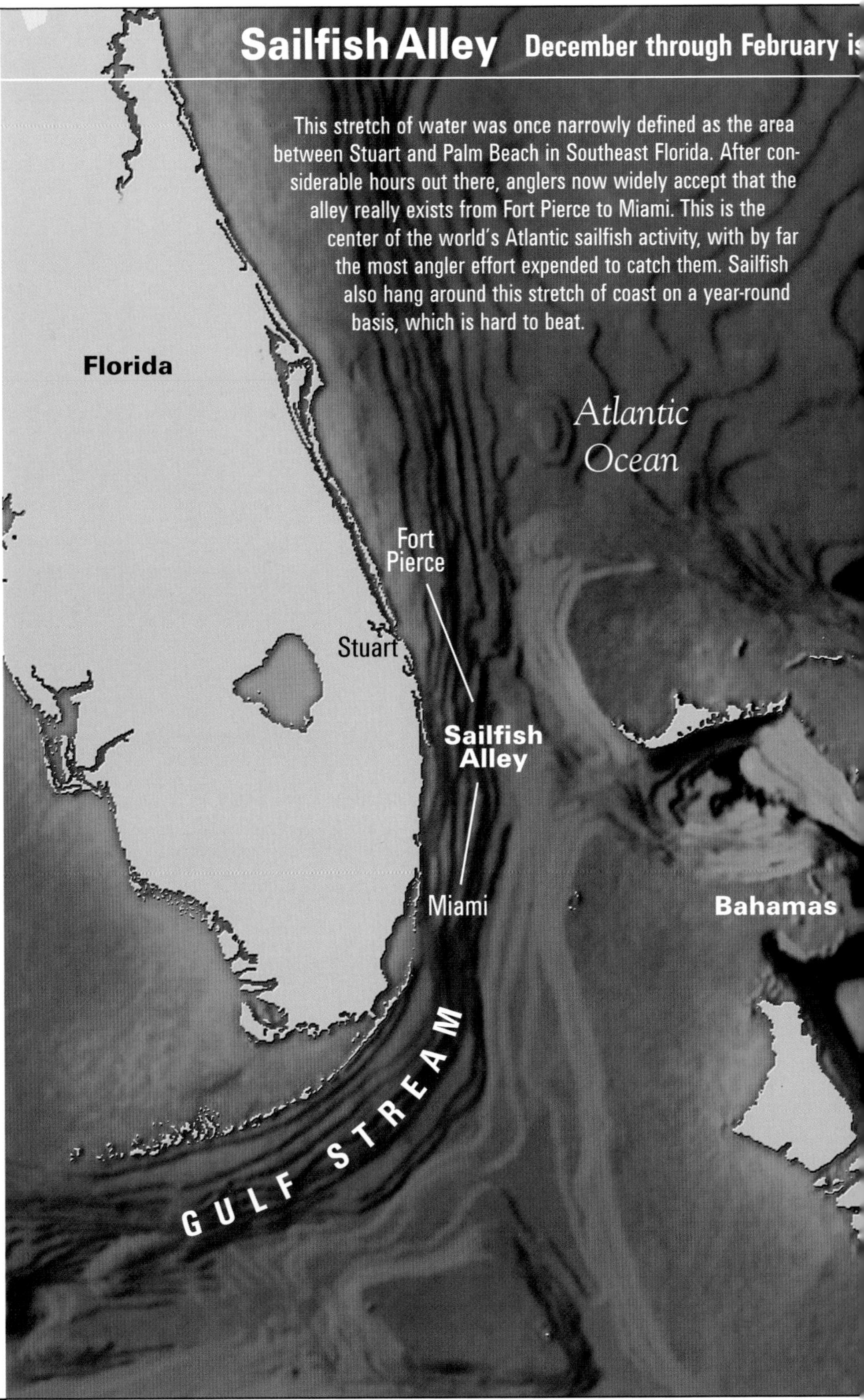

**Florida**

*Atlantic Ocean*

Fort Pierce

Stuart

**Sailfish Alley**

Miami

**Bahamas**

GULF STREAM

During summer, the southern edge of these migrating fish can be found here while in late winter the northern edge of the fish are still around. It's during the middle of the run, December through February however, when you'll find an absolute gridlock of sailfish "right out front."

This expression implies that the fishing is extremely close to shore, and that's just the case. From Stuart to Miami, you'll usually find the best water and most of the fish a scant one to three miles from the beach. Sometimes, these fish hang around for days in only 40 feet of water. For this reason, combined with a locally high concentration of bluewater anglers, the Alley in winter is perhaps the best stretch of any coast to see sailfish.

This winter fishery revolves entirely around two factors: cold weather and baitfish availability. The cold will get the fish moving south, and the food supply will hold them until the next cold front pushes them south. This is also the point where boats make the switch from deadbait trolling to live baiting. The high-density population of anglers, easy accessibility to small boats, tournaments and the fact that tourism is peaked out all contribute to intense angling pressure on these fish.

Early season here is best for fast action; a noticeable lack of aggressiveness with sailfish has been observed after a heavy tournament weekend. Plan your outing here for December or January and you won't be disappointed. Watch for a break in the weather, which isn't difficult in

South Florida, and it's not unusual to see anglers release a double-digit catch of sailfish from flats boats.

Raising release flags off Sailfish Alley, where the South Florida coastline is heavily populated.

On a calm day, anglers in flats skiffs score multiple sailfish landings.

## Gulf of Mexico

This is certainly a huge body of water and the fact that most of it is inaccessible to recreational boats is a consideration. All five Gulf States enjoy a population of sailfish of their

**The waters around Cancun, Isla Mujeres and Cozumel have long been a hotspot for sailfish.**

own. From Texas, Louisiana, Mississippi, Alabama and the west coast of Florida, boats fish offshore during summer and regularly catch sailfish. The limiting factor here is the long distance required to reach blue water.

Calmer summer weather on the Gulf Coast means that outboard-equipped boats can catch billfish and other bluewater species safely. Sailfish that make their way north into the Gulf during summer spread out over a huge area and are frequently encountered well within range of small boats. This same pool of sailfish are likely the same fish found off Mexico's Yucatan Peninsula during winter and spring.

Boat crews trolling blue water in the Gulf during summer can expect to mix it up with sailfish along with the usual dolphin, wahoo and tuna. Covering a lot of water is important to locate these fish. However, if you come across an area where more than one sailfish is raised, consider slowing down and pulling some small, rigged ballyhoo at an easier pace. You may be surprised to find all the action you can handle with these Gulf spindlebeaks.

## Mexico/Yucatan

This venue definitely deserves mentioning, since this is where the sailfish run terminates to the south. The combination of Atlantic and Gulf fish colliding here during winter and spring is amazing. The waters around Cancun, Isla Mujeres and Cozumel have long been a hotspot for sailfish. Not many years ago, this was a remote destination with little fishing pressure. No longer; it's now a premier destination for large U.S sportfishing boats to take extended vacations. The reason is obvious: Great concentrations of sailfish are available, often within a few hundred yards of reefs and sunny beaches.

On any given day from January to April, you may find enough vessels here to rival the Palm Beach fleet. Don't fret, however: The sailfish bite here is still remarkable, despite an army of talent chasing these fish. Dozens of releases each day are common and fishing dead ballyhoo around numerous pods of fish balling sardines may leave you bored of catching them before the trip is finished. Mexican authorities have clearly realized what a valuable contribution these fish make to their economy and smartly banned the use of live bait here. One can only imagine the temptation of backing up to bait pods all day, hand-feeding sailfish live baits. That would make for a fabulous day of action, but the number of gut-hooked fish would probably not be worth it. **SB**

# The Bahamas

This island chain should not be overlooked. Though not traditionally thought of as a sailfish destination, the "islands" definitely play host to plenty of them. Sailfish are found here throughout the year and many visiting anglers from Florida (on their own boats) are often afforded multiple chances at sailfish during their stay.

The Bahamas hosts a series of tournaments each year for billfish (the Bahamas Billfish Championship, or BBC) where marlin are the primary target, but many sailfish are caught in these events, to round out the scoreboards.

Sailfish are caught here during the winter as well and often go unmentioned. These catches coincide with Florida's Sailfish Alley run of mid-winter. Winter is when angling pressure is the lightest in the islands, due to weather limitations when cold fronts arrive. It does, however, raise the question of how much east-to-west movement is part of the sailfish migration route. SB

Sailfish prowl in The Bahamas, just like anywhere else. These fishermen run a classic Bertram boat south out of Long Island.

# CHAPTER 15

# Flyfishing: Central America and at Home

**M**any sailfish enthusiasts, after landing countless fish on bait, add various new challenges to their program. If you've never tried it, catching a sailfish on fly involves plenty of extra effort. The added effort and lesser odds for success will ultimately give you a greater sense of accomplishment while adding a more advanced angling approach to the sport as a whole. This is taking offshore fishing to the next level to be sure.

Before you tackle this lofty goal at home, a visit to the tropics is an excellent way to tune up your game. Multiple shots per day at sailfish on the long rod are common south of the border. This amount of practice offers you the chance to sharpen your skills and will ultimately make you more prepared to try it on your local population.

**If you haven't tried a sailfish trip in Latin America, give it a shot; it's great!**

Pacific sailfish average much larger than those in the Atlantic, and these big guys are often caught in calm water that lasts for weeks. As it turns out, they also love brightly colored flies, providing fabulous action.

# Southern Latitudes

**S**ailfish from both the Atlantic and Pacific oceans are becoming increasingly popular targets for fly anglers. One common reason why more anglers are trying them on the long rods is the increase in "destination fishing" abroad. As the sportfishing world branches out to more remote locations and new fisheries emerge, you notice a trend. At first, a few pioneer anglers, at some expense, travel to remote waters in search of unspoiled grounds to fish. As they invest in these devel-

## With many chances to get it right, fly anglers love it here.

Catch a 100-pound sail on fly and your day is made.

oping areas, discovering their bounty, word travels fast and before long more people travel there and another hotspot is born.

Before you know it, these newly discovered remote and exotic destinations have developed an infrastructure capable of handling tourist trade. That once-remote fishing spot is suddenly open to anyone ready to fish even a long weekend. One prime area is Central America on the Pacific and the Yucatan Peninsula of Mexico. The Pacific coast of Mexico, Costa Rica, Guatemala and Panama offer some of the most plentiful sailfish in the world. The key word is numbers (shots per day) and that's what it takes to make flyrod sailfish a reality.

All of these locations have numerous local and U.S. boats working hard to provide visiting anglers more shots at sails than you can imagine in a single day. Luxury resorts have sprung up at most of the popular destinations, providing all of the creature comforts on land and unparalleled angling in relatively calm waters. While not specifically designed with the fly angler in mind originally, more of these outfits have turned to fly fishing for plentiful sailfish.

A common scenario here is that anglers

The billfish fleet from Crocodile Bay in Costa Rica, ready for a day's action offshore.

become bored with catching so many sailfish on standard tackle. It can be hot work, after all, and these fish can become almost a nuisance when searching for marlin. This sounds like a problem most of us would love to have, but it happens. To add more challenge, the fly tackle comes out. Inexperienced or even first-timers with the long rod get a real hoot at actually landing billfish on fly. That's when conditions are right—and they often are. These venues offer calm days when dozens of sails are raised and baited in a single day. You have many chances to get it right. That's why fly anglers love it here.

What is it about these hotspots that makes them so fertile? Like anywhere you'll visit to chase fish, the key ingredients are plentiful food and light fishing pressure. Unspoiled waters in southern latitudes teem with baitfish and billfish, which frequently rise to the surface to feed.

Pacific sailfish are dark and grow quite large. This one prowls in the engine wash, ready to pounce on the first baitfish it can find.

# On the Fly

**A**fter a day of wearing them out on trolled baits, try changing your tackle and teasing them up with bait, then switch to a fly.

Let's start with tackle. Captains Ron Doerr, Butch Constable and Raymond Baird are three knowledgeable Florida flyfishing guides, who

make annual pilgrimages to Costa Rica for sail fishing. For them the tackle is simple. As experts, they agree that a No. 13 to 15 weight rod and a large arbor reel, capable of holding 400 yards of 80-pound Spectra backing, is a smart choice. While it may be feasible to land

sailfish on fly tackle. It's accepted that ulti-mately, you'll find yourself under-gunned with anything smaller than this. For fly lines, an intermediate or sinking line is preferred over floating lines. The reason why floating lines are not favored is the tendency for buoyant, popping flies to skip along the surface in the breeze. Other lines give the fly stability and help them track more favorably, making it eas-ier for the fish to catch them. Leaders are pretty simple, as well. Captain Doerr prefers using loop-to-loop connections for building leaders, for both speed and ease when the action gets fast.

He has also crafted a pretty nifty technique for building sailfish flies, which makes a lot of sense. This fly (page 201) solves the problem many anglers experience when trying to stick the hook in a charging billfish. The traditional flies used are double-hook models with a sliding foam popper pushed down to the head of the fly. With this arrangement, when the fly stops, the hooks sink and the fly takes on a vertical attitude, making solid hooksets more difficult.

As far as techniques are concerned, it's very simple. Combinations of three teasers with hookless baits are trolled on the surface until a sailfish is raised. One of the outriggers is kept lowered to accommodate the three lines, while the second outrigger stays up and out of the caster's way. The right 'rigger is raised up for a right-handed angler and vice versa. Your choice of lure/bait combos is pretty big, but bird teasers are very popular in the calm waters

> It takes a big fly reel and a 12- to 15-weight "rhino rod" to catch a Pacific sailfish, that easily reaches eight feet and longer.

off the Pacific coast. They're trolled in conjunction with a softhead lure and strip bait or ballyhoo. The three baits are staggered at 20 feet back for the short line, 40 feet for the middle bait, and 60 to 100 feet for the long bait. Standard procedure involves trolling around an area where bait schools are located until one or more sailfish are raised into the spread.

When a fish is spotted in the baits, that bait is cranked in, away from the fish. With the engines in neutral, your fly angler replaces the bait with a fly. A dialogue must be maintained, of course, between the person removing the bait and your angler. It's critical to find a comfort zone for the angler, so he's able to present his offering and keep the fish interested. One common foulup in this plan occurs when the mate removes the bait too quickly. Or he teases the fish too close to the boat to work the fly in front of it. Captain Doerr suggests a distance of 20 to 25 feet as ideal range. This distance makes it simple to get off an easy 40-foot cast that keeps the shooting portion of your line off the rodtip. A few quick strips will straighten out the line.

Once the sailfish shows interest in the fly, all it should take is a few well-timed strips to make the popper chug on the surface. When the sail charges the fly, your rod should be low and pointing toward the fish. For efficient hook-setting, these guides also suggest being

patient. While you may be tempted to "rare back" and bend the rod, it's better to let the fish take the fly and turn away from the boat—before coming tight with the line. Pulling the line while the sailfish is pointing toward the

# The Captain Doerr Fly

Captain Doerr's fly is tied on a piece of stiff clear plastic tubing with a foam rubber sleeve slid over its center. Feathers forward and aft of the foam center make up the collar and tail of this squid pattern fly. With the center section being buoyant foam, and the foam popper for a head, this fly floats level in the water. All that's needed to complete your offering is a pair of 7/0 or 8/0 cutting point livebait hooks, such as the Owner model, snelled together with 80-pound mono. Simply slide the popper and tubing onto your shock tippet and tie on the tandem hook rig.

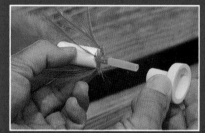

The finished product. Pacific sailfish often jump on these imitation baitfish flies like they're starving.

angler usually results in a missed shot. Captain Doerr has found that letting the fish move off for a few seconds, in effect dropping back, and clearing the loose fly line briefly works best.

Familiar 31-foot Bertrams and sailfish near rocks rising from the water means you're very likely in Panama.

The fish will hang on to the foam body of the fly for longer than one would think. While the fish moves away from you momentarily and your extra line jumps off the deck, the angle of the fish increases the likelihood of a solid hookup. With a set of stripping guards or a glove, simply grab the fly line and stop it

momentarily, stretching out the line and planting the hook firmly. This move is close to foolproof, once you get the hang of it. Next, let the fish go and enjoy the show. When the fish is finished with its initial panic run, you should get on it fast. These guides suggest using five pounds of drag on the reel, but also using subtle hand pressure on the spool to crank up the heat when possible. Avoid lifting the rod and pumping too dramatically. Or "high-sticking" or changing angles a little too frequently.

If this sounds like your idea of a big time, try visiting any of these destinations between December and April for the best action. A trip to these fertile waters is a great chance to pack a lot of exciting experience into a short amount of time. This will make you a better angler and more adept at dealing with those limited bites back home.

It's possible to catch a sail on fly in your home waters, if you take advantage of opportunity when it knocks.

Unfortunately, you can't expect many daily shots at sailfish back in the States. There are some days, however, under "ice cream conditions," when the fly rod can score in local waters. Knowing when you have a realistic shot and being ready are the keys. For starters, it's necessary to carry a fly rod at all times. The chance this condition will happen with any advance warning is slim, unless a winter sailfish run is in full swing during good weather conditions. Provided you have the tackle ready, here's what to look for.

To get the sails fired up right behind the boat where you can see them, add a daisy chain of live baits with no hooks in them. This rig is easily made by tying a series of dropper loops, two feet apart, with a small snap swivel at the end of each dropper. Tied on 80-pound mono with up to nine drops on the rig, this is a quick rig to get a bunch of live baits in the water for teasers. After you've jigged up a good supply of baits (cigar minnows and Spanish sardines are very good), bridle one for each swivel, one at a time with a loop or rubber band through their eye sockets and place them in a bucket of water.

After completing baits for each swivel, hang each bridled baitfish on a swivel and send them out on a trolling rod. Resume bump-trolling around in loose circles over the pods of bait. It's important to keep moving ahead slowly, to prevent live baits on the teaser from tangling. A string of big cigar minnows swimming strongly in perfect formation just below

the surface is quite a temptation. Once a fish is raised to the teaser, take it away from the fish and replace it with the fly. Your fly should obviously resemble the local bait.

For this to be successful, you must have your fly line ready to go in the water right away. Before you set out, make a cast behind the boat and strip your line into a five-gallon bucket. Leave the rod in the corner of the transom in the ready position with the fly hanging on the edge of the bucket. Your angler should be ready to go at all times, ready to act. These chances happen fast and won't last as long as they do in other parts of the world. For the most adventurous who are willing to give it a shot, catching a sail on fly in U.S. waters is a real challenge—and a feat that few anglers can claim. **SB**

When sailfish are concentrated around large schools of bait, preferably in fairly shallow water of less than 100 feet, you should be ready. Fishing over bait pods is an ideal setup for fly-fishing, since sooner or later these sails will rise to the top. To get the odds in your favor, commit to throwing only the fly at them. You'll never catch one on a fly if you keep throwing live baits with hooks attached. Start by trolling slowly in circles around the bait pods with your dredge teasers in the water. This will bring the fish closer to the surface, but usually not close enough to chase a fly.

# CHAPTER 16

# Conservation

It takes very little interaction with sailfish in their natural environment to realize what a valuable renewable resource they are to anglers. Simply put, the net worth of such a magnificent animal simply cannot be measured by the pound. Unfortunately, we live in a society of inflated and ever-increasing costs.

As the already developed economies of many nations expand and over-exploited ocean resources deflate, the need for new sources of revenue takes its toll. Billfish, a once highly revered gamefish, have in some places been reduced to nothing more than a cash crop. The downside of this is that unlike acres of corn, which are harvested and replanted each year in the same field, there are no farmers out there planting billfish.

**Billfish, including sailfish, are the ultimate marine fish worth protecting from commercial harvest.**

It only takes a few minutes to drag a sailfish along by the bill, to help revive it. This forces water through the gills, building up oxygen in the fish. The bill should be held close to the mouth to avoid any damage to the point.

Action at sea: water invades the deck temporarily, while backing down hard on a fast sailfish.

# Saving Sailfish for Tomorrow

An alarming trend has been noticed in the Pacific Ocean and the outlook could be bleak for billfish populations and a growing sport fishery, if this trend continues. While a billfish management plan was enacted in Atlantic waters to protect all billfish other than swordfish from sale, this is not the case in the Pacific. The hitch in this fishery is that some of the best places to catch billfish in great numbers are just offshore of some very underdeveloped countries. This fact makes it easy for a commercial longline operation to wave ready cash in the face of people pulling the strings, in exchange for fishing rights.

You may have seen the pictures and heard the stories of sailfish and marlin stacked like cordwood on some dock, from a friend just returned from Central America. I can tell you I have seen it myself and the stories are true. The fact is, these billfish Mecca resorts won't be all that attractive once the billfish are gone. Monetary funds injected into these economies by visiting sport fishermen benefit more people and last a lot longer than funding gained through the sale of fish. While it may seem like this is a problem you can do very little to solve, the very least we can do is express our disapproval. If you are fortunate enough to visit one of these locations such as Costa Rica, Guatemala or Panama, for example, you can certainly make it known why you were attracted there. You may also make it

clear that tourist dollars will last much longer than money brought in by longliners, who ultimately disappear with the billfish, often back to their home port across the Pacific Ocean.

This is really a problem of such magnitude that it might seem like there is little that can be done to prevent it. On a global level, the sad truth is you're probably right, except for joining some billfish conservation group. Other than in our own waters off the Hawaiian Islands, where billfish are still killed and sold, it's very difficult to influence international fisheries policy. However, we can certainly control what goes on in our own backyard and especially behind our own boats.

This should begin with an examination of our own fishing behavior. Not too long ago, it was common to see dead sailfish on the docks being held up for pictures. The catch-and-release philosophy had not yet taken firm hold; most anglers responsible for the killing didn't have a clue. Slowly, however, the con-

Back in the "good old days," happy crew with dead sailfish in Fort Lauderdale.

cept of catch-and-release caught on and fewer people killed their billfish for bragging rights. Eventually, any sportfish crew who threw a dead sail on the dock became unpopular.

The last holdouts that continue to kill sailfish regularly today are a part of the charter fleet trying to sell taxidermy. Since no part of your actual sailfish is ever used in a mount today, it's absolutely unnecessary to keep a fish for a mount. The dead fish simply becomes a bargaining chip to leverage a potential taxidermy customer, who has second thoughts about pulling the trigger on a mount. The charter crew that still does this may not want you to know about it. They know by now that most anglers are happy to release a sailfish and have a fibgerglass mount made.

Replica mounts, which have been the industry standard for many years now, have become a lasting art form and the proof is in the final life-like product. Awareness of your options before you leave the dock on a charterboat will eliminate any confusion when a leader is coming up to the rod tip. You might also explain your intentions to a crew before you sail on a charterboat and explain to them that you would or would not like to mount a fish, but killing one is unnecessary. The more people that become aware of the process of creating a taxidermy mount, the better for the fishery. (See the taxidermy chapter).

Another area of the sport fishery that cer-

# Tagging Fish for Science

The method most effective in tracking the movements of migratory fish has traditionally been the responsible tagging, releasing and subsequent recapture of these fish, and this is going to be the only way we can accurately determine their range. There are two tagging programs to participate in:

### Cooperative Tagging Center
### NMFS/NOAA
Southeast Fisheries Center
75 Virginia Beach Drive
Miami, FL 33149

### The Billfish Foundation
2161 E. Commercial Blvd, 2nd Floor
Ft. Lauderdale, FL 33308

It pays big dividends to proceed as quickly as possible, and get the tag into the fish without beating the fish up in the process. And obviously the healthier the fish around the boat, the more likely it will be recaptured later with a tag.

When you set out to tag a sailfish, have everything ready at the time of hookup, and assign each person a specific task: for example, one person to leader the fish, one to plant the tag, and one to record information about the fish and its capture as it happens.

Having a crew capable of performing like a well-oiled machine is important to the survival of the tagged fish, and since the rate of return is so low with billfish (less than two percent), it's imperative these fish are released in very good condition.

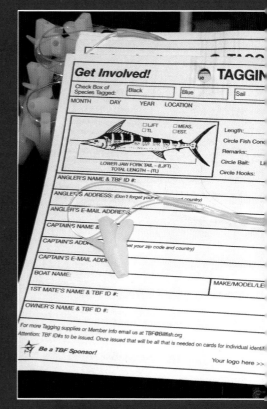

The best way to determine sailfish migr
tions and manage them is to tag an
release, a practice now widely accepte

tainly takes a toll on sailfish stocks is tournaments. Tournament fishing for sailfish, while using an all-release format, still puts a strain on local populations. Again, this may not be a popular opinion but it's the truth. When dozens of boats all fight it out to release as many fish in the shortest amount of time, there are inherent flaws.

The main cause of injury or death to a sailfish in this situation is rough handling on the leader. Since the final outcome is influenced by the number of releases, mates have the tendency to either "pop" the fish off by yanking

on the leader or simply cutting away a tired fish without reviving it. The extra time it takes to revive a fish or cut the leader close to the hook could cost you points. With large cash and your reputation on the line, it's too

Broken-jaw sailfish, fighting hard during tournament action. Did the mate pull too hard on the leader?

easy to get on to the next bite and forget about the one you just had. This is short-sighted, when you consider the long-term effect.

Taking the most talented sailfish crews in the fishery and turning them loose on a concentration of fish for a few days results in lots of catching. For instance, the 2006 Silver Sailfish Derby in Palm Beach saw 986 sailfish released in only two and one half days of fishing, by exactly 50 boats. This kind of action, while very exciting, can take a toll on the fish. However, it's up to us as stewards of the fishery to be responsible for the health of the fish we target. Whether changing the rules for release tournaments to revive each fish if necessary will make a difference, I don't know. (Many boats have high gunwales, for instance, making it difficult to reach the water.) These

**You can start by taking every measure to ensure the survival of a fish you intend to release, by catching them on the right tackle.**

fish certainly deserve another chance, after bringing them to boatside.

The use of circle hooks for sailfish is also becoming mandatory in many tournaments. While this may seem like a step in the right direction, don't be misled into thinking you can't hurt a sailfish with a circle hook. Remember to treat both J-hooks and circle hooks alike in the way you drop back to a bill-fish. For a few reasons, most people have a great deal of difficulty hooking fish on circle hooks when they begin using them. The main reason for this is the age-old habit of hauling back on the rod and striking the fish, which is difficult to change. Yanking on a circle hook is not going to work. In my experience, the first thing anglers do to overcome this flaw is feed the fish (free-spool) longer. You'll see it happen until the dropback seems to go on forever. Ultimately the fish swallows the bait and you gut-hook it. Don't let anyone tell you it doesn't happen with circle hooks; it happens all the time. Whether or not you elect to use circle hooks is less important than how you use them. Fished properly, they can be a useful conservation tool.

A captain could go on for days about who's helping and who's hurting the fish population. Longliners, charterboats, tournament anglers or just the uninformed weekend boater, whoever is more to blame aside, what can you really do to make a difference? You can start by taking every measure to ensure the survival of a fish you intend to release, by catching them on appropriate tackle, landing them as quickly as you can and taking extra care with them at the side of the boat before cutting them loose. It is also our responsibility to educate others along the way. Take the time to explain why it's important to treat the fish a certain way to your fishing partners and discuss with them how fish are going to be handled on your boat. Take time to introduce others to the sport and help educate them along the way. Take your neighbor or a friend fishing. A person who otherwise might not have the chance to go fishing on the ocean can be a great addition

Tired but happy anglers after an amazing day on the water. That's a lot of sailfish release flags.

NO PROBLEM
SINGER ISLAND

to your crew from time to time. And of course take a kid fishing. Taking a rookie out and catching them their first sailfish is a very rewarding experience. Seeing the excitement in a first-timer's eye, as they catch a sailfish, is almost as much fun as doing it personally. Seeing a kid catch their first sailfish is better than doing it personally.

More importantly, try to look at every bill-fish you are about to release through the same

Protecting sailfish stocks for the next generation means teaching young anglers about conservation.

eyes you saw your first one with. That sense of pride and accomplishment should not diminish with each passing flag you raise on the outrigger. After you've caught hundreds of sailfish, remember they're still the same highly evolved, beautiful predator that first caught your attention. With that in mind, handle them with the respect they deserve, so that our oceans and fish will provide you with memories to last a lifetime, and a legacy for future generations. **SB**

## Doing Your Part

To get involved in billfish conservation, one can gain a sense of empowerment by joining one of several marine conservation organizations, who often lobby for sensible harvest quotas—when not protecting bill-fish from harvest entirely. The following groups are recommended:

### TBF
The Billfish Foundation
(800) 438-8247
(954) 938-0150
fax: (954) 938-5311

### CCA
Coastal Conservation Association
(800) 201-FISH
(713) 626-4234
E-mail: ccantl@joincca.org

### RFA
Recreational Fishing Alliance
(888) 564-6732
(609) 404-1060
Fax: (609) 404-1968
E-mail: joinrfa.org

### IGFA
International Game Fish Association
(954) 927-2628
Fax: (954) 924-4299
E-mail: hq@igfa.org

### NCMC
National Coalition for Marine Conservation
(703) 777-0037
Fax: (703) 777-1107

# CHAPTER 17

# Sailfish Taxidermy

**H**aving a real artist as taxidermist makes a big difference in the long run, when building a fish replica to commemorate a treasured moment from a memorable day spent offshore. Fish wall mounts today are built to last, since they're made of plastics, fiberglass and the latest paints. It's the artist, however, who adds the finishing touches. Obviously, someone with a trained eye and experience helps, as well as sheer talent.

It's often artist versus factory worker, when measuring quality and beauty in fish "taxidermy." Older fish mounts made from real fish (and their skins) years ago tend to fade, darken, crack and even leak fish oil. They're now mostly found in bars and museums. Some of the work going on today with newer technology can only be described as beautiful art.

**Art versus an exact replica: Which looks better and lasts longer?**

Real sailfish or molded and painted art? Some of today's "taxidermists" can create a fish so life-like, they could jump off the wall or sit on the cleaning table, waiting to be filleted.

# Space-age materials

Old-fashioned, skin mount trophies have long fallen from fashion, since they require the fish be killed. In addition, skin mounts seldom last longer than 20 years and begin to first discolor and then disintegrate, because they're a combination of organic material from the fish, mixed with paints and plastic.

A replica of the fish made from a combination of modern, non-organic materials will actually last hundreds of years if taken care of,

**The public is more aware now, and fewer fish are being killed and wasted. In the early 1980s the skin mount business shut off.**

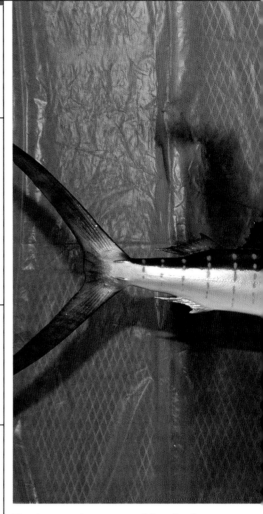

especially if they're not dropped and the fins broken. Technology today allows for casting these fish in mixtures of urethane, acrylic and fiberglass, among others. There are all sorts of "cool" plastics available.

"Fiberglass has come a long way," says artist Mike Kirkhart at New Wave Taxidermy in Stuart, Florida. "We can even do clear fins on some species, such as spearfish and flying fish. We do realistic mouth interiors, belly slits, gills, color on the back side of the fish, you name it. Acrylic paints have come a long way. There are also water-based paints, safer for people. New composite materials have improved. I can make hand-made acrylic eyes, for instance. It can take an entire day to make two eyes for a large billfish."

New Wave is one of several taxidermy firms offering innovative replica mounts.

"Sailfish are spectacular and make beautiful mounts," Kirkhart continues, "and I really enjoy doing them. Reproductions (from skin mounts) are just what they say they are.

Taxidermy is the name we fall under, but our name means a new look. We left the market of skin mounts a long time ago in 1977, and that's why we call it New Wave, a different direction."

The public is more aware now, and fewer fish are being killed and wasted. In the early 1980s, the skin mount business pretty much shut off. Even skin mount taxidermy companies realized it was cost effective, and switched to reproductions. Kirkhart molded real fish years ago, and picked up the natural features with an artist's eye. He has around 100 molds from real sailfish, doing mainly three poses— dorsal fins laid back, dorsal spread out, or the so-called "tail walk" pictured above. He also has special sailfish, though he doesn't advertise them. They're twisted, contorted and painted

The finished product, just before the second coating of acrylic is applied, to make it look wet. They don't get any better than this.

on both sides. They're certainly more expensive, maxing out at about 20 bucks an inch, but very beautiful.

These molds are not just some idea of what a fish was like—they're the exact thing made from fish that died. The problem, Kirkhart says, is that sometimes the public still thinks they have to kill a fish to get that realistic effect. With 100 sailfish molds, Mike can closely match length while the angler's fish can be released alive. Some people even call him for a sailfish mount, folks who haven't even been fishing or maybe they lost a nice one after a battle. The same holds for other species. You could order a great white shark to hang over your living room, for that matter. All it takes is a credit card number and delivery address. After the economics of the purchase is over, most people want something beautiful. You're collecting art, instead of just getting one of those reproductions.

"We're seeing fish mounts made in China now, at a discounted rate," says Mike. "The decision is whether you want something made from the other side of the world that looks okay, or do you want something beautiful? Everyone is different. We don't do black backs with only one eye, for instance. Some people do prefer that cheaper option, however. The price range for fish is somewhere between $10 to $20 dollars an inch, as a rule. The more you pay, generally, the higher the quality."

There are fish sculptures, too. Miami International Airport had New Wave build and put up 500-plus fish in geometric shapes. They worked in conjunction with artist

Donald Lipsky from New York. It was quite a job and took a year and a half to make all the fish and put them up, after airport construction delays. Everyone who sees it really seems to enjoy it, especially international fishermen arriving in Miami. There are probably four sailfish arrangements, with about 25 fish involved. It's in Concourse D, which means some people miss it when they're in other parts of the airport.

"These mold fish mounts are the way to go, if you want people to stop killing sailfish, which still goes on," he says. "There are captains out there who still whack sailfish for a commission from taxidermy shops. That's putting a bounty on a fish's head. On the dock they may tell customers that the fish was boated for their benefit so it could be mounted—even though that fish will be thrown in a dumpster and a reasonable facsimile made from fiberglass.

## Painting the Mount

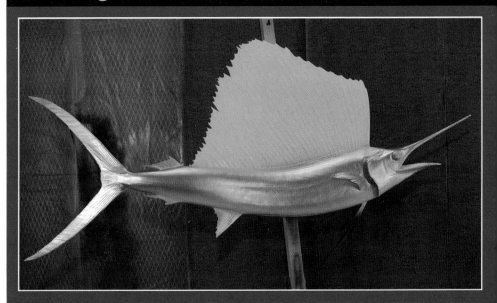

Unpainted mold above is coated with silver paint, to make it glow from underneath. Then Mike Kirkhart applies the first layer of paint. This requires years of experience and a gas mask, of course.

Suddenly the angler is paying a lot of money for his fish. I've been against this for years, and don't do this style of business from dock captains working on commission, that's just taboo. This old custom of high commissions is slowly fading away, thank goodness. The Internet has certainly helped us work more independently with the customers. We get inquiries from all over the world, make nice high-end pieces of art and business is good."

It's unfortunate that any charterboat crew that still kills these fish (to guarantee a nice commission check) is allowed to continue to operate. Their charterboat business and our children's sportfishing future is being compromised for a bounty. Let's not support this nonsense. Back in 1989, Deb Kirkhart came up with the New Wave company motto:

"Catch for the thrill, release for the future, mount for the memory." **SB**

Shades and shadows are applied with black, with the fish's eyes taped over for protection.

Black spots are painted on, one at a time. This requires a steady hand.

Fins underneath are sprayed, with the background along the fish's sides protected from more paint.

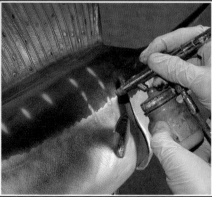

Neon blue is added last. This is optional, depending on how much you want that fish lit up.

## MAGS

### Sportsman's Best Inshore Fishing

How to catch your favorite shallow water fish.
- Techniques
- Tackle options
- Tips from the pros

Includes DVD with great inshore action. **$19.95**

### Florida Sportsman

Published monthly for Sunshine State anglers. Includes bonus coverage of the Caribbean.

### Sportsman's Best Snapper & Grouper

First in series of informative how-to books. Includes 60 minute action packed DVD. **$19.95**

### Shallow Water Angler

New from FS. Published quarterly for skinny–water fishermen from Maine to Texas.

### FS Lawsticks

Now, also; Texas, Louisiana, Mississippi, Alabama, Georgia, North Carolina, South Carolina, Virginia and California.

Folding plastic **$4.95**
Clear Mylar **$3.95**

ALL-COLOR
### Annual Fishing Planner

Florida tides & monthly tips. Know when and where to catch more fish. **$8.95**

### Fishing Charts

24 regional Florida charts covering inshore and offshore. Includes GPS, boat ramps and fish ID.
**$14.95 each**

### Wall Calendar

Fine art for your home or office. Each month has different art. Includes holidays, moon phases and seasons. **$11.95**

**Call: 800.538.7347 or Order Online www.floridasportsman.com/store**

- Order FS Items
- Subscribe to FS
- Weather
- Fishing Forum
- FS Fishing Shows
- FS Radio Network
- Today's Casts
- Weekend 4cast

# SAILFISH DVD

Sportsman's Best: Sailfish DVD brings the written pages of this book to life. George LaBonte and the editors of Florida Sportsman travel through "Sailfish Alley," fishing and talking with some of the best sailfish experts out there, to bring you one of the most informative, comprehensive and exciting DVDs ever produced on sailfishing.

## FEATURES
- ► THE WORKING MAN'S BILLFISH
- ► ROD AND REELS
- ► LINE AND LEADERS
- ► TERMINAL TACKLE
- ► TEASERS
- ► OUTFITTING YOUR BOAT
- ► LOCATING SAILFISH
- ► READING THE WATER
- ► KITE FISHING
- ► DRIFT FISHING

## SPECIAL FEATURES
Exclusive interview and footage with Ray Rosher and the *Get Lit* team after their record setting 35-fish day.

## DETAILED BAIT RIGGING
- ► Wedge Head Split Tail Mullet
- ► Skipping Ballyhoo
- ► Split Bill Ballyhoo
- ► Ballyhoo Circle Hook Rig
- ► Perfection Loop w/Strip Bait

"Whether you're an experienced angler or looking for your first sailfish, this DVD is for you. It covers all the bases, giving you the information you need, from getting started with your basic set-up to outfitting your tournament winning boat."
**Publisher, Blair Wickstrom**

DVD Executive Producer: Paul Farnsworth
DVD Production Assistant: Matt Weinhaus